THE GAMES PEOPLE PLAY

THE GAMES PEOPLE PLAY

Sam Keery

Book Guild Publishing
Sussex, England

First published in Great Britain in 2012 by
The Book Guild Ltd
Pavilion View
19 New Road
Brighton, BN1 1UF

Typesetting in Baskerville by
Keyboard Services, Luton, Bedfordshire

Printed in Great Britain by
CPI Group (UK) Ltd, Croydon, CR0 4YY

A catalogue record for this book is available from
The British Library

ISBN 978 1 84624 732 3

Contents

The Games People Play

There are two kinds of games: the physical ones such as football or boxing, and the thinking ones such as chess or bridge. The physical ones can again be divided – into those needing youth and fitness such as football and those, like golf, which can be played by anyone, even into old age. But they all have one thing in common: they are all highly competitive. However, this competitiveness is supposed to be conducted with fairness and honesty. It is called sportsmanship. Public schoolboys once had the inspiring example held up to them of the great cricketer W.G. Grace. When the umpire had ruled him not out on an appeal by the bowler for being run out, Grace contradicted the umpire, saying that he had indeed not quite crossed the line of the crease and so was indeed out. Grace is up there with the youthful George Washington who could not tell a lie. They are both examples of sportsmanship. The phrase 'it's not cricket' is still applied to anything in any business that is not strictly according to the rules.

Rules. In some games these are very simple and need little umpiring. In games with individual competitors it is usually fairly obvious which one is the winner. But then there is handicapping. This has the seemingly noble intention of giving every competitor an equal chance to win. So in a running race the slowest start before the fastest; in archery the best bowman is furthest away from the target; in golf the poorest players tee off with starting points already on the board. But then look what can happen if the handicapping is spot-on correct. Suppose that to be the case when a world-class player helps out a local club by doing a charity round with the locals. If the champion wins, it would not get a mention in the news. Why should it? But what if the handicapping allows some local A.N. Other to beat him? Headline sensation! Of course it would never be allowed to happen. Sportsmanship has its limits.

Still on golf, we had the wonderful (in the entertainment sense) Tiger Woods episode. Tiger Woods, a sporting role model for boys who clamoured for his autograph at matches; almost the W.G. Grace of golf, he was so famed for his sportsmanship. Exactly what happened is disputed. His car crashed into a tree after coming out of his driveway. An ambulance was summoned. The police also arrived, though it is not clear who summoned them. His wife was at the car, a golf club in her hand, claiming she was trying to break into the car to get her husband out. The car seemed undamaged, unlike Tiger Woods, who was unconscious from a head injury. It is unclear how he came by this inside a locked car. It was suggested he was clobbered while making his escape from the house and just managed to get into and lock the car before succumbing to the injury. It is said that the police wanted him to bring charges but he refused because of what would emerge. Which emerged anyway: his extramarital women. First one was identified, then another, and then another. Did it stop at six or were there more? All the leading comics now did a Tiger Woods act. One included a fake golf club wrapped around his head under his hair to make it seem it had cleaved his skull. When the women count reached six, the acts included appeals for women to come forward who had *not* slept with Tiger Woods. But something else came out that did his role model image far more damage than his bedroom behaviour – his golf course behaviour when doing practice rounds on local courses.

Golf course behaviour is less a matter of rules than of

etiquette, in which respect it can be more gentlemanly than cricket. Thus when a faster player comes up behind a slower they should shout 'Fore!' to warn the player in front about the danger of being struck and the slower should respond by allowing the faster player to 'play through'. But when the Tiger Woods party came behind a player his minders did not shout 'Fore!' but 'Get out of the way – it's Tiger Woods'. If his ball arrived on a green with a player already on it, his party would take the ball out of the way of the great man's. However, although this behaviour had been known for years, if a sports writer even hinted at it, his paper would be threatened with a withdrawal of advertising – so powerful were the Woods PR people. But when the news of his wife flooring him with one of his clubs hit the headlines, the taboo was broken. Worshipping fans no longer assembled at the eighteenth hole for his autograph. The sporting icon had fallen off his pedestal. Today he is simply one of a sizeable number of world-class players.

Golf is not the only sport in which an alternative use can be found for the implements used to hit the ball. When a man who had led a sheltered life went to watch his daughter play in a hockey match he was appalled by the sheer viciousness of what the players did with hockey sticks – one of the captains was stretchered off with bleeding shins. His daughter did not see why he was shocked.

Croquet might seem the least likely to be another one. Players, who are invariably of the higher social orders, use mallets to knock balls through hoops on greens in country houses. Nothing could be more sedate it would seem. But the rules allow a player who cannot themselves win to stop another player from winning. This can result – as happened in a game that made news even in the tabloids – in not only the police being called but an ambulance in which more than one player was taken away. What impressed most was that the green was at a vicarage!

Then of course there is the beautiful game itself. Football. I will not attempt to explain the offside rule. Occasions when penalties are awarded for infringing it are the subject of controversy. A recent one in a very important match that was televised caused arguments in half the households in the country, not least because the referee was a woman – which, the two top TV commentators paid millions for their expertise said, was the reason she had got it wrong. How could a woman be expected to understand the finer points of a man's game, except that subsequent slow-motion replay studied by experts showed that, although close to borderline, she had been right. But at least she did not have to be escorted to the dressing room by a cordon of police to avoid injury from fans invading the pitch after an offside ruling, as happened once at a cup final qualifier. The police included two mounted on horseback.

Then there are the school football matches in which some fathers take a rather keener interest than the school would like. One father turned up at every game in which his son was playing to shout advice to him from the touchline. And not just to his son, and not just advice, but to the referee. It was decided something had to done after a game in which the referee happened to be the headmaster. The school came up with what seemed the obvious solution – drop the boy from the team. What that resulted in is somewhat confused as reports about what happened came mostly from the boys, and boys have a tendency to exaggerate. While it is plausible that there was shouting and a commotion in the corridors, it is hard to believe that the science teacher brought the boy's father down with a rugby tackle or that the headmaster locked himself in his study with a chair wedged under the door handle, until the police arrived.

But it is not only fathers of players who take the beautiful game very seriously. There was the young woman whose father was a fanatical supporter of Tottenham Hotspur. He did not know how to break the news to his wife that he had got out of his daughter why she had kept putting off bringing her new boyfriend to meet them. Oh God, his wife said, he hasn't put her in the family way, has he? Oh no, her husband said grimly, it's far worse than that – he's not only an Arsenal supporter, he's in the fan club.

Then there was the man interviewed on TV who claimed that the most important day in his life was the day England won the World Cup. He was a man in his sixties with grandchildren.

And what of the non-athletic games? Well, I understand that bridge players are advised not to partner wives or husbands at tournaments as this can lead to domestic violence or even divorce. Let us return to games with individual competitors. I once heard a man speak with great feeling at how shocked he had been when a friend took him to an all-in wrestling match, and the worst of the shouted comments came not from the male spectators, vociferous though the were, but from a group of elegant-looking women in ringside seats: 'Break his back! Screw his leg off!'

What about the gladiators in the Roman Empire? Some became rich and famous. Their perks included being taken into the beds of patrician ladies. There is a scandalous story recorded by one of the Roman writers studied by schoolboys doing Latin – though this story is not in the school textbooks. It is about the quarrelling of – call them – Lady Hoity-Toity and Lady Toffee-Nose over one of them pinching the other's gladiator and causing scenes at the coliseum.

It may be objected that many of the gladiatorial combats were rigged. But the spectators wanted to see blood and the gladiators let them have it. If you had been a gladiator, you would have wanted to be confident that your opponent could nick veins and not arteries with exact precision. So in rigged fights the spectators were being presented with a demonstration of swordsmanship probably more skilful than in non-rigged ones.

Then there were the chariot races. When the Empire split and the eastern part became Byzantium, somebody there had what seemed a good idea at the time. It was to make races no longer for individual competitors but for teams. So, instead of a single umpire at the finishing post, there now had to be umpires all along the track awarding penalties for obstructing and so on. And, as well as that, the teams each attracted huge numbers of fans who sat together in the arenas and indeed began to be from particular suburbs - rather like Glasgow Rangers and Glasgow Celtic football clubs. And, just like Rangers and Celtic fans, they did not always agree with the decision - based on penalty points - on which team had won. They disagreed most memorably on one occasion when violence in the arena became rioting in the city and the army had to be called on. Before peace was restored, over a thousand people had been killed.

It couldn't happen today, could it? Well, just a few years ago in South America in an Argentina vs. Uruguay game the pitch was invaded by fighting spectators and before order could be restored over one hundred rival fans were dead. Guess what caused it? An offside decision.

The offside rule was discussed - if discussed is the right word - in a packed pub bar watching the Cup final. Someone other than one of the fans innocently asked why the offside rule couldn't be got rid of: why couldn't a player kick the ball anywhere on the pitch regardless of who was beside him or behind him. Well! He was soon put right! The offside rule was what made football the great game it was, providing the very means by which anybody in a pub watching TV can become an expert in challenging the most borderline decisions. This great country of ours wouldn't be the same without it.

The Rangers vs. Celtic rivalry referred to above has, of course, a Protestant vs. Catholic side to it imported from the politics of Northern Ireland. During the Troubles there a visiting American couple who were stopped at a paramilitary roadblock thought they could ensure their safety by saying they were atheists. But, they were asked, are you Catholic atheists or Protestant atheists?

1066 and All That

After the Norman Conquest the Norman overlords of England sent their sons to France to keep up their French. However, after about a century this policy began to run into trouble. The sons began to have experiences similar to that of a young woman from South Africa who once worked in my office. She was called Marietta Sneyman and as her name indicates, she was an Afrikaaner. Her first language, Afrikaans, which I heard her speak on the phone to her mother, was a version of Dutch brought to South Africa by the first settlers in the seventeenth century. But modern Dutch has changed since then, as she found out when she visited Holland, just as the later Normans in England must have found out the hard way that French had changed since 1066. The poet Chaucer mentions this in *The Wife of Bath's Tale*:

Full French she spoke and well did know
But not the French of Paris but of Stratford-Atte-Bow

The English Normans' experiences in visiting France must have been as unhappy as that of Afrikaaners visiting Holland. Marietta's Afrikaans must have sounded to the Dutch rather like what the biblical English of the Pilgrim Fathers who first colonised America would sound to us. Were their tongue still spoken in some part of America, an American girl on a visit here would, like Marietta in Holland, cause much amusement with her thee-ing and thou-ing. Maybe the later English Normans would have been as outraged as

Marietta was if their French hosts had done to them what the Dutch did to poor Marietta. They brought the neighbours in to hear her! It must have greatly dampened the English Normans' enthusiasm for trying to keep up their French.

In France after 1066 once-powerful regions like Normandy lost out to the Paris region whose version of the French language gradually became the standard for the whole country, making Norman French a regional dialect. Meanwhile, in England the Normans' initial history-making triumph at the Battle of Hastings was not bringing about the cultural transformation they must have intended. While the modern English language that slowly evolved after 1066 certainly contains many words of Norman French/Latin origin (French originated as a regional dialect of Roman Empire Latin), it is still largely Anglo-Saxon. It is now thought that the unhappy experiences of the later English Normans in being laughed at for their country yokel sounding French must have speeded up their adoption of the language of the conquered country and so curtailed the influence of Norman French on the evolution of English. Perhaps they took out their resentment at this upon the evolving English language by what they did to Anglo-Saxon words like 'shit', 'fuck', and 'cunt', turning them into nasty insults and obscenities when they had been simply the ordinary Anglo-Saxon words for excrement, copulate and vagina.

I have learnt that there is a fairly reliable rule for identifying words with Anglo-Saxon roots other than the swear words. They are usually short words with no obvious French or Latin association. Start with some of the key words necessary for the speaking or writing of English: *Who, what, when, where, how ... and, but, if, or, of, on, it, to, from ... now, then, up, down, under, over, above, below ... after, before, never, ever ...* and many more, *all* of them of Anglo-Saxon origin. And the others? Well, look at the text on this page. While there are certainly more than a few words of Norman French/Latin origin, the majority are of Anglo-Saxon origin, as would be the case with any other page composed by anybody or in any printed page.

Norman conquest? What Norman conquest?

But maybe we should give the Normans a bit of credit for other things they brought here – the Norman warhorse, for example. Hollywood movies got it all wrong depicting knights in armour mounted on beautiful racehorses. When the Normans developed chain mail and armour they needed very strong horses to bear the weight – the horse was armoured, too. So, by repeated selective breeding over many years, they developed the huge animals which, in England, transformed the landscape when the Anglo-Saxon peasants and yeomen used them to pull the plough instead of a team of oxen – the latter are still used in India and the East. Up till comparatively recent times they were a common sight on our streets and roads, hauling huge loads such as barrels of beer to our pubs.

Today, of course, these horses are bred only for show. But what a show! I went to one once. When the first of them was led into the arena – I cannot remember if it was a Shire, a Clydesdale or a Suffolk Punch – it got a bigger murmur of admiration from the spectators than would the most beautiful racehorse. It was a magnificent creature. A mother asked if her little girl could pat it. Of course she could. And give it a lump of sugar, which it took very delicately from the little girl's hand and then gave her a friendly nuzzle.

So what had come over with the Normans as a fearsome armoured war machine was now a gentle giant nuzzling a child, and, as I looked on, I remembered my own childhood when coal was delivered on our street and we children gathered round the great carthorse to pat it, quite unfrightened by its size. So it was not only in our wonderfully rich, mongrel language that the Anglo-Saxons tamed the Normans.

Social Class and Accent in England

When the British prime minister Margaret Thatcher first entered Parliament she took elocution lessons to get rid of her slight northern accent. That was because England is the only country in the world with a country-wide middle-class mandarin accent considered socially superior to all its regional accents. In, for example, Germany, a politician from Bavaria would be expected to speak in a Bavarian accent; an Italian from Sicily would be expected to have a Sicilian accent. The Kennedy clan in the United States, the nearest thing to an aristocracy America has produced, came out of the Harvard, Yale or Princeton colleges with their Boston East Coast accents intact. My wife has a half-Spanish daughter by a first marriage whose childhood was spent in Asturias in northern Spain. When I asked her if that region had a distinct accent she said that everybody hearing her would know she was from Asturias. When I then asked her if, say, well-off people would look down on her Asturian accent she was puzzled. Why should they? she asked. Why indeed! Yet I remember a fellow from Taunton in Devon being puzzled in the opposite way when, in my naivety, I asked him why he did not have a West Country accent. He said something about having had a good education. He obviously thought it perfectly natural that only the uneducated would have the accent of his region. Then there was another fellow who, hearing my Belfast accent, told me proudly, 'I'm an Ulsterman, too,' in a plummy English accent no doubt acquired from spending half his childhood and all of his youth at boarding schools in England.

Of course there was a time when the English mandarin accent ruled beyond England, though, oddly, not on its borders in Wales or Scotland. In Scotland up till the nineteenth century the judgements of the Law Lords were delivered and printed in broad Scots (Robbie Burns' language) as was a version of the Bible. Half of Wales speaks Welsh – the British prime minister Lloyd George's first language was Welsh. Hence the Scottish and Welsh middle classes, like their American counterparts, have regional accents that are respected at all social levels. But Ireland was very different. In a very amusing TV series called *Some Experiences of an Irish R.M.* there was no need for the actor taking the part of the R.M. (resident magistrate) to have an Irish accent since in real life he would, being Anglo-Irish gentry, have had an English public-school education.

Ireland has changed since then. James Joyce went to a top Irish private school (until the money ran out) and, although living in Europe, he went on to speak perfect French and – it is said – purer Italian than the average Italian and was the greatest wordsmith the English language has ever produced; he spoke English with a distinct Dublin accent. By his time, the moneyed Irish no longer sent their children to expensive schools in England but to expensive Irish ones and consequently, like Joyce, they kept their Irish accents. However, in British Northern Ireland the old ways persisted. Louis MacNeice, the famous poet, was born in Belfast. But, being the son of the Bishop of Connor and Dromore, was educated at Marlborough public school and then Oxford, thereafter living in England. He did a lot of radio broadcasts, in which neither he nor the BBC saw anything incongruous in him forever parading his Irishness in an English public school accent. The BBC and British cinema reinforced and indeed extended the sway of the mandarin accent by replacing the *ah* sound with *eh*, so that, for example, a phrase such as 'A man's hand' was pronounced 'A men's hend'. You can still hear this prissiness in clips from old movies and broadcasts. It has mercifully passed and indeed the BBC tried for a time to allow the news to be spoken in a mild Yorkshire accent by a famous northern radio broadcaster, Wilfred Pickles, but stopped it when it was found that even northerners preferred an accent they 'could look up to'.

This English accent snobbery started up comparatively recently historically. Sir Francis Drake, the great seaman at the court of Queen Elizabeth, spoke with a broad West Country accent and all the other knights and indeed nobles at her court would also have brought with them their regional accents. William Shakespeare would undoubtedly have had a Midlands – Brummie – accent. Samuel Johnson – called the patron saint of the Conservative Party – was from Yorkshire and would have pronounced the words in his great dictionary with a northern accent, and we know that the poet Keats had a London accent from his out-of-London detractors exaggerating it in their sneering at him as *Cockney* Keats.

The English mandarin middle-class accent appears to have evolved with the great expansion of the public schools in the early nineteenth century. These had begun in the Middle Ages as charities to provide an education for the deserving poor to be literate servants; indeed, they still get tax exemptions as charities and attempts by governments to abolish this absurd anomaly are routinely frustrated by so many MPs having been to them. However, something of their early origins still survived in their great nineteenth-century expansion which came about from the burgeoning British Empire needing officials to run it. These were drawn from not particularly well-off middle-class families to fill posts that were not particularly well paid, as we learn from the 1930s writings of the Old Etonian George Orwell who was born in India into such a family, though by then of course the rich had largely taken over the public schools. But in their early days there must have been a trend to iron out the boys' regional accents to provide the imperial officials they were to become with a standard accent. This then spread to all of the English middle classes where it became regarded as *no accent* – only the lower orders have accents! Consequently, the English are all able to place each other in the social order from their accents.

There has been some shift in recent years. Self-made millionaires no longer have such a chip on their shoulders about their regional accents, though they send their children to 'good schools' to get rid of any trace of Geordie, Brummie, Cockney or Scouse.

In America and most other countries, class distinctions are dictated in a more brutally simple way – *money*. But in England the accent-ridden class system is more akin to the Indian caste system in which a hard-up high-caste Brahmin can feel himself entitled to look down his nose at a lower-caste millionaire in a Rolls-Royce.

As George Orwell would have put it, that's England for you – keep the aspidistra flying!

The Decline of the Left: The Light that Failed

It is easy to forget that there was a time when the left wing was powerful everywhere in the world except America, where it was, and still is, anathema. America is the only country in the world where both the main political parties are right wing and even the most militant trade unionists leading strikes are anti-socialist.

In Europe, just after the Second World War, there was a huge swing of public opinion in support of left-wing parties. In this country the Labour Party was elected on a landslide, fuelled by returning servicemen no longer prepared to put up with unemployment, means-testing for the dole, slum housing and having to pay to see a doctor. Labour brought in the National Health Service, its lasting legacy to this day.

Some of this leftward swing was due to admiration for the Soviet Union and the heroic Russian people. But it had already started in the 1930s when the Labour Party had become big enough to be joined by ambitious politicians, not all of them, however, entirely happy to join in the singing of 'The Red Flag' at party conferences.

The 1945 Labour landslide was a stirring event even in Northern Ireland where I was a teenage boy. I still recall the excitement that seemed to be transforming the normal Catholic nationalist versus Protestant unionist divide. Protestants were going into the polling booths to vote for Labour Party candidates alongside Catholics.

It would be an exaggeration to say it was similar to what

the young poet Wordsworth reported about Paris in the opening days of the French Revolution: 'Bliss was it in that dawn to be alive and to be young was very heaven.' But I well remember my father on election day rushing in from the garden to listen open-mouthed to the latest poll results on the wireless and then rushing out again to shout them over the hedge to our neighbour. I recall the cool voice of the BBC man saying repeatedly the names of constituencies '... Labour ... Labour ... Labour ...' and my mother telling him: 'Either dig your garden or cheer on the election! Look what you're bringing in on your feet.' (It would be an even bigger exaggeration to describe the later backsliding of people like Wordsworth into crabbed old reactionaries who opposed reforming child labour and workhouses as being like the Labour Party's abandonment of nationalisation.)

But that came later. The 1930s and 1940s saw a great burgeoning of the left wing in this country and in most of the world except America. In Europe the communist parties attracted such huge support that in Italy, for example, they nearly became the biggest party. Even in this country communism nearly became respectable. The communist paper the *Daily Worker*, while not peddled on the streets outside stations like the main papers, was stocked at shops inside the stations. There were even some pinstriped businessmen on commuter trains who would open a copy of *The Times* to peruse discreetly a *Daily Worker* inside it. The championing of the Soviet Union by the Dean of Canterbury was not only tolerated but earned him the almost affectionate title of 'The Red Dean'.

So when and why did the tide start to turn?

There was the business of the Soviet–Nazi pact at the outset of the war which the left does not like to be reminded about. When Hitler invaded Poland in 1939, he and Stalin agreed to let Russia occupy the eastern half, and for the first eighteen months of the war when Britain was fighting alone and in danger of invasion, Russia was supplying Germany with valuable war materials. This caused consternation and division among British communists, some of whom had fought in Spain against the German-supported fascists. But, when Hitler invaded Russia in 1941, this was immediately forgotten. Communist shop stewards in factories who had been half-hearted about supporting what the Russians had previously denounced as a 'capitalist' war put their backs whole-heartedly into war production now that their beloved Soviet Union was itself in danger. All Britain rallied in support of the heroic Soviet Union. Mrs Churchill headed the Aid to Russia Fund, to which everybody gave something. Stalin was pictured affectionately as 'Uncle Joe'.

It did not last. Even before the war ended, the West was alarmed by the Russian conquest of eastern Europe and the setting up of satellite communist governments. Soon after the war Churchill spoke of a new 'Iron Curtain' dividing Europe. Within a few years there was an arms race involving nuclear bombs and rocket bases. The North Atlantic Treaty Organisation was set up to confront the threat from Russia. The 'Cold War' came into being. Communist parties everywhere declined in membership. In this country taking the *Daily Worker* was no longer respectable.

But the first great watershed event was, of course, the uprising against communist rule in Hungary. The year was 1956. Film clips are still shown on TV depicting Russian tanks smashing trams aside in Budapest and firing upon demonstrators. The extreme left wing in this country was shaken to its core, but claimed that the uprising in Hungary was the work of 'counter-revolutionaries'. However, a reporter from the *Daily Worker* who was sent to Budapest to confirm this caused consternation by coming back sympathetic to the insurrectionists. The Communist Party was in turmoil with big-name resignations.

Yet there was also a rallying of support for the Russian intervention, not without some success. This was helped by the widespread outrage at the simultaneous British/Israeli invasion of Egypt after the Egyptian president, Nasser, nationalised the British-owned Suez Canal and took over the British-run Canal Zone. There were huge demonstrations in Trafalgar Square denouncing this act of imperialism. It divided the country. Friendships were broken, families divided. I recall a hospital visit when a group around a bed opposite were arguing so loudly that nurses asked them to stop as they were disturbing other patients.

But Suez distracted attention from Hungary. The *Daily Worker* survived, as did the Communist Party, though with reduced membership. Extreme left-wing members of the Labour Party kept their heads down even more.

But the biggest watershed was very different. It was what happened at the 26th Congress of the Communist Party of the Soviet Union. Nikita Khrushchev stunned the delegates – and indeed, the world – by denouncing Stalin, whom he himself had served under. He spoke of Stalin's reign of terror in which no one was safe, in which he and others, right up to the top, had never known whether they would get the midnight knock. He told them of how Stalin's bloody purges of army officers in the 1930s had nearly caused Russia's defeat in the war. He spoke of the possibly millions who had perished in the terrible labour camps.

This bombshell was shattering not only to communists but to the left wing everywhere. It is hard today to appreciate the effect this had on the left wing in this country, especially those who had lived through the 'hungry thirties'. To them the doctrine of 'From each according to his ability, to each according to his need' was a sacred text (and indeed it is as beautiful as the biblical Beatitudes). And the Soviet

Union was, they fervently believed, actually striving to bring this about. To them, Russia was a great light shining in the eastern sky, heralding a future for humanity free from want and oppression. They had visited the Soviet Union as worshipfully as Muslims making the pilgrimage to Mecca. They had refused to listen to accounts of the Stalinist terror, branding them lies peddled by the hyenas of Fleet Street, the jackals of the bourgeois press.

But now the Russians themselves were saying to them – in effect – 'Comrades, all those lies were true!' This was devastating. Mass resignations reduced the British Communist Party to the size of an obscure sect. The *Daily Worker* became about as important as the Salvation Army paper *The War Cry*. In Europe the membership of the once-mighty Italian and French communist parties plummeted.

But it was not only communists who were badly damaged. The British Labour Party felt obliged to ditch what had long been disliked by its more right-wing members – Clause 4 of its constitution: public ownership of the land and the means of production. Even the word 'socialist' became unfashionable. Today the Labour Party is no more than slightly left of centre, while a resurgent Conservative Party attempts to dismantle anything publicly run – even the National Health Service.

In Russia itself, the very birthplace of the October Revolution, we see the almost unbelievable spectacle of multi-millionaire 'Oligarchs' buying up what had once been huge state industries. We have come a long way since the exciting days of Keir Hardie and the first cloth-capped working-class members of Parliament, the days when all Europe seemed to be about to turn to socialism, when 'from each according to his ability, to each according to his need' shone like a great light for humanity. The light that failed.

Brushed by the Wing of History

The mass breakout of IRA prisoners from the Maze Prison in June 1983 made an exciting day for the citizens of Old Warren housing estate in Lisburn on what were once Lagan river fields across from Blaris. A crowd gathered to watch the RUC and the Army fish escaped IRA men from the reeds. A van with chimes arrived to sell ice cream. Teams of London newspapermen arrived to record the words of those with a story to tell. The *Observer* interviewed a taxi owner whom I went to school with. A prison officer in the town had engaged his taxi with great urgency - except that he was not a real prison officer at all... My old schoolmate spoke feelingly of what it is like to be caught up unwittingly in the whirl of historical events, to be brushed by the wing of history.

Well, I have news for him. He once had a much bigger brush with history and involving that very spot - what is now the Maze Prison. He once lived in one of the few remaining thatched cottages in the area looking across the river fields to Blaris. If he cares to read a thick book setting out the records of Hitler's meetings with the German High Command, he will find that in January 1941 the generals got out their maps and guided Hitler's pointer to RAF airfield Long Kesh - which would become the Maze Prison - and the long river fields nearby.

I thought we knew then all the things for which those river fields - or river meadows as the Germans called them - had evolved over the ages: they were for the summer pasturing of cattle; for Sunday gambling schools; for courting couples; for the exercising of greyhounds; above all, for the pursuits of boyhood. But it seems they were also suitable for the landing of German fighter aircraft. They would have landed very near to my old schoolmate's cottage.

The fighters would have landed with nearly empty tanks after escorting the paratroop transports. With a bit of luck they might have taken off again with captured fuel from Long Kesh. Hitler was a great believer in luck – like Napoleon with whom he was always comparing himself. Napoleon would always enquire of an officer recommended for promotion 'But what of his luck? Is his luck good?' In 1941 Hitler's luck was still very good indeed.

A paratroop attack on Northern Ireland was not the German High Command's first plan for a diversionary invasion of Ireland in support of the invasion of Britain which was code-named Operation Sea Lion. This had been postponed in September 1940 because of the failure to destroy the RAF in the Battle of Britain before the autumn deadline and was now set for spring 1941 with a much beefed-up Luftwaffe and before the attack on Russia code-named Operation Barbarossa. Hitler was set on invading Russia at all costs, but he still thought he could invade Britain, too, and it was touch and go whether his will would prevail over the more doubtful High Command.

The plan for the invasion of Ireland was code-named Operation Green. Hitler would probably have bawled them out over the first plan for Green. When British Intelligence later got hold of it and passed it on to the Irish military, they could hardly believe it was serious. Open barges towed by tugs to Wexford. Some with horses in them! Heavy guns mounted on the bows. If they had ever got to Wexford and been fired, you would have been safer on the Wexford beaches than in the barges – especially the barges with horses in them! Hitler might have enquired sarcastically if there would be an ice-cream van with chimes. He could be very sarcastic with people. Reichsmarshall Goering, head of the Luftwaffe, was still sulking and boar hunting at his castle after the hurtful things Hitler had said to him after the Battle of Britain.

Clearly the Irish business did not get the best brains. They were all on Barbarossa and Sea Lion. Well, not quite all. There was a Colonel Kurt Student of the 11th Airborne Corps. Had a bee in his bonnet. Would not take no for an answer. Upset his superiors by approaching Hitler over their heads. At Obersalzburg on New Year's Day 1941, Hitler made the High Command listen to the Student plan for Operation Green: Northern Ireland, not Southern Ireland; Northern Ireland airfields vital for protection of British Atlantic convoys ... paratroop attack to capture airfields; RAF would have to divert fighters ... draw off British fighters long enough for Sea Lion to establish bridgeheads at Brighton and Eastbourne ... parachutist transports and one-way Messerschmidt 109 fighters ... Long Kesh airfield ... river meadows at Lisburn.

Hitler was enthusiastic. He liked boldness, dash, speed, surprise, *blitzkrieg*. He would have liked the cheek of the Messerschmidts filling up again at Long Kesh, as when some of his tanks had raced ahead of supplies in the blitzkrieg into France in 1940 and had pulled in to fill up at French roadside petrol pumps. This was a blitzkrieg man after Hitler's heart (and, indeed, in the summer of 1941 Colonel Student's paratroops conquered Crete in just such an attack on airfields as he had proposed for Northern Ireland). Hitler would have ordered the High Command to prepare the operational road and street maps. Get Goering here! Napoleon was right! One should have faith in one's destiny! How Hitler loved his maps, his Wagner, his destiny.

I wonder what we were doing when Hitler's pointer landed on those Lagan river fields of boyhood. There was much we were happy not knowing at twelve years old. When German bombers blitzed Belfast in May 1941 – 300 of them on the heaviest raid according to German records – we were happy not to know that the bits of schrapnel we passed around with the smell of explosive still on them represented terror and death. We were happy to speculate excitedly that ours would be the next school to be commandeered to shelter the bombed-out 'refugees' as we called them, who streamed out of Belfast with belongings piled on lorries, horse carts, donkey carts, handcarts, prams, anything with wheels. I was happy that my beautiful Belfast cousin was a refugee at our house where we nearly became lovers, but I was not sure what to do. We need little at twelve to make us happy.

Those of us who have never fully adjusted to not being twelve any more should study all the ages of man set out in the 'Life Tables' of the insurance companies where it is found that the age at which the human male reaches his peak (least likely to die) is – guess what? Yes. Twelve. Just before puberty. After that (sex, girls, women…), it is downhill all the way.

I doubt if my old school chum or any of the rest of us would ever again be so happy as on those Lagan river fields, as oblivious of the precariousness of our world as the cattle that came down to drink in the cool of the evening like in a painting by Constable. In those wartime boyhood skies of cloudless blue we saw no shadows, heard no faint beating of that dark wing which surely hovered over us, before, seeking larger prey, it wheeled toward Barbarossa and passed us by.

Men's Fashions

There are two quite different aspects to changing fashions that apply to both sexes. One is identifying an historical period from the clothes worn in paintings. Whatever the range of individual variations – austere, flamboyant, simple, outlandish – they all have something in common that identifies them as belonging to a particular age or epoch or century. The other is the sudden 'catching on' of a craze that may be just as suddenly dropped – for example the 1920s cloche hats for women, spats or plus-fours for men.

Here I am referring only to the changes in more recent seemingly established fashions.

Boys used to wear short trousers. The shorts had to be above the knee. Boys would have rows with mothers who, as they got older, made them wear hand-me-downs from older brothers that went below the knee – shorty longs – which got them jeered at in the playground. There was a transition to long trousers at about the age of eleven. This was an important rite of passage from boyhood to youth. Boys would row with mothers who delayed it, causing more jeering from their peers. Today, of course, boy's shorts are a distant memory.

Until comparatively recent times, boots were worn by the entire working class and quite a few of the middle class. My father was a bespoke shoemaker, yet in the photo I have of his small shop the sign above it says 'Boot Maker'. Today boots are worn only by the military or those who do very heavy jobs. When the working classes took to wearing shoes just before the Second World War, boots went the way of boys' shorts into history.

In an aerial photo of a football cup final in the 1920s you see a sea of caps. You will not find a single bare head. Caps because football then was a working-class pastime, but while it would have been soft hats at outdoor middle-class gatherings such as for cricket or horse racing, the same would have applied – no bare heads. However, move forward to the 1930s and similar photos would show many bare heads. But the change did not come about without resistance. There are stories of bare-headed men on the streets being stared at or made the subject of hostile remarks. We find it hard to understand why what we would think of as simply a fashion should have been so socially obligatory that for men to be bare-headed in public almost bordered on indecency. Today the only reminder of the age of obligatory headgear is the schoolboy's cap.

Until recently when men went to the barber's they were automatically given a short back and sides, hair brushed to one side with a side parting and with or without hair cream. About the only variation was the hair brushed straight back with a middle parting, but this was considered a shade racy, the sign of a ladies' man.

The controversy about which Scots regiments wore shorts under the kilt took on a new lease of life a year or two ago with the discovery of a Roman clay tablet near Hadrian's Wall near the Scottish border. It was in fact a letter from a Roman mother to her son. Initial admiration for the Roman army's postal system – the mother lived in what is now Romania – gave way to wrangling over the things she listed in a parcel which presumably accompanied it. They included underpants. This caused an outbreak of angry disagreement among Roman scholars, some of whom had believed that Roman soldiers, like true Scots, did not wear any. But they did not give up easily, insisting that this particular Roman soldier was molly-coddled. If so, he must have greatly missed his mother on one of the toughest postings in the Empire, and it is hard to believe that he would have risked derision by being the only one in his unit to wear underpants.

When did men's underwear start? We have a rough idea about women's from a story about women horse riders. Forget side-saddles – they were an invention by the prim Victorians with their prudish views on what was ladylike and were, in any case, only used on ceremonious occasions – women straddled saddles and threw their legs over to mount just like men. But this was before jodhpurs or women's trousers. So grooms at inns were very helpful in offering horse-riding women, especially good-looking ones, their cupped hands to put a foot into for a leg-up. It may be that this thoughtfulness had something to do with the fact that – how shall I put this? – the fashion for women to wear knickers had not then caught on to anything like the extent it has today.

But why did it take so long for men's knickers – which is what most underpants actually are – to arrive, though a lot of men still wear boxer shorts. (Mercifully, they have stopped wearing the hideous ankle-length long johns, which, on washing days, used to balloon out beside their wives' knee-length bloomers to the embarrassment of teenage sons and daughters for whom their disappearance into history could not come soon enough.)

Whatever happened to the nightshirt? Why was that easy-to-put-on and take-off simple garment replaced by pyjamas – jacket, trousers, flies, tie ribbon? Have you ever accidentally pulled out the tie ribbon and tried to thread it in again? Or, having had a lie-in with a hangover after a night out, answered the door bleary-eyed without your dressing gown, and your pyjama flies open, causing the woman who has called to flee with a shriek? There's none of that with a simple nightshirt. So why are the few men still wearing this sensible garment considered eccentric?

Then there are ties. The old school tie. The regimental tie. Unwanted Christmas presents passed on the following Christmas. At one time worn with a high-winged collar by politicians and the judiciary. They are still so widely worn, albeit more casually, that it might seem silly to ask if they are on their way out. Yet there are ominous signs. A prominent politician recently appeared on the telly in a smart lounge suit and an open-necked shirt. In the not so distant past that would have been deemed unthinkable. The TV people would not have allowed him to go on the air like that. Leading restaurants would have refused him admittance. Even when the move to open-necked shirts with lounge suits began to take off, men in open-necked shirts on dinner dates carried ties in their pockets in case they might be required wear. But now they are simply a matter of majority choice and no longer obligatory with even the smartest of suits. I hope I don't sound like a hide-bound old colonel spluttering into his gin and tonic at his club if I ask, 'What next? Silk scarves and buttonhole flowers with jeans and trainers?'

America: A More Foreign Country Than France?

An English couple were in the news recently. They had moved to America because of his job, after living in France for some years. But they left America after about six months and were reported as claiming that it was because they found America a more foreign country than France. This caused a bit of a stir in the news, with people on both sides of the Atlantic calling their claim rubbish. I was a child in the 1940s, the golden age of Hollywood, when we went to the movies at least once a week, used American slang in our street gangster games and in accosting American wartime GIs with 'Got any gum, chum?', swapped American comics with each other, enjoyed Bing Crosby and Frank Sinatra on the radio, and later read books by Hemingway and Scott Fitzgerald. Then there were the times when American politics – the McCarthy persecutions of anybody left-wing, the presidential elections, the assassination of JFK and so on – seemed as important to us as our own politics. So why did I, too, not immediately dismiss as an absurdity the idea that America is a more foreign country than France? What was niggling at me to think about it?

The first thing that came into my mind was something I thought I had long forgotten. My father's brother, my Uncle Billy, lived in New York and came over on a visit just before the Second World War. I have only the vaguest memory of it – chiefly of the great black cliff with portholes in it which was the liner in Belfast Lough when they saw him off again. But my older brother remembered him more clearly and when, after the war, he was sent by his engineering employers to New York for some reason, he thought he would look him up. But the visit was not entirely happy. Those were the post-war years when the British Labour government introduced the National Health Service. To my brother's surprise, Uncle Billy and his family, all working class, had a go at him about it. They hoped Northern Ireland was not going to go socialist like England. He said they spoke the word 'socialist' like it was a nasty disease.

I will return later to what we know of the American health system. But before that I will go back to that couple who prompted this article and the order in which they described the differences in American culture which they could not get on with, starting with their arrival in a small Midwest town where the man had got a job. Things began well it seemed, when a group of neighbours called to welcome them. But when the Americans thought the couple might like to be told of all the churches in the town so that they could worship in one of their particular denomination – Baptist, Presbyterian, Congregational, Anglican and so on – there came a chill in the atmosphere when the couple said they were not religious. The Americans were shocked. The couple were in small-town America where not just many people, but *everybody* went to church on Sundays. The couple had thought that this was a feature of European Catholic communities but this was a Protestant town. They were discovering that Protestant America takes belief in God so much for granted that the people in this town had never before met an unbeliever and reacted to this as to something unnatural. Yet should the couple have been so surprised? I thought of the televised speeches of President Obama and the frequency with which he invokes God: '. . . before God . . . under God . . . with God's blessing . . . if God wills it . . . in our prayers . . .' And he does this obviously assuming that it would seem perfectly natural to his American audience. No European politician, however privately devout, would make speeches like that.

Then their American neighbours spoke admiringly of our Royal Family, thinking the couple would be pleased, and were taken aback to be told that the monarchy meant nothing to them. The Americans found it hard to believe that any English people could speak so disrespectfully of the Queen and the princes. In the somewhat chilly conversation about this and the couple's contempt for the Bush presidency, which they had wrongly expected the Americans to share, the couple were surprised to discover how deferential to authority the Americans seemed. Could these be the same people who had thrown off British rule and set an admired example to the world of standing up to tyrants, of not bending the knee, unlike the forelock-touching British who still harboured traces of feudalism?

But then another memory came back to me of the only occasion when I had actually met Americans other than the wartime GIs as a child. It was when I was a head of department with the Prudential Assurance Company. A group of Americans from America's biggest insurance company – Metropolitan Life of New York – visited us. It was because their company was introducing flexitime (a clocking in and out system) already in use at the Prudential and they were worried – if it was good for the company, was it good for them? They were being shown around by my deputy, Norah, who happened to be the head of the trade union branch to which the staff now all belonged – one of the many changes that had taken place in the company since I had joined it many years before. She was able to reassure them that both sides benefited – while the staff now had to make up time lost if their train was late, they could work longer hours and save it up to take days off. However, she was surprised at their reaction to what they saw of our working conditions. When I had joined the company, departments had been like school classrooms with the desks in rows and the head of department sat at the front like a stern teacher. Now the head of department had a small office and the staff arranged their desks any way they liked, some sporting flowers and potted plants, and strategically placing filing cabinets and cupboards to give themselves a bit of privacy. They left the room without having to ask for permission, sometimes coming back with a coffee from a vending machine in a corridor. But it seemed that at Metropolitan Life it was still like it had once been at the Pru. Were the Americans envious? No, quite the contrary. They did not approve; indeed, in my department, she said they had been shocked. Shocked? At what? Well, it was when I and some of my staff were explaining something to them and my staff had addressed me by my first name and not, as they would have had to do at Metropolitan Life, by 'Mister' or even, in the case of the most junior, 'Sir'. Norah said that those Americans had changed her idea of stuffy English vs. free-and-easy Americans, indeed had turned it on its head!

The couple in America had also been struck on first arrival by every front lawn of the attractive clapboard houses on their street having the American flag on it, and in being given one to put on their own lawn to replace the one taken away by the previous occupants. They had caused surprise by asking if this was because somebody important was about to visit the town, perhaps even the President? No, the flags were there all the time. It was their first but not their last encounter with how patriotic Americans are. This prompted another memory of mine to surface. It was of the experience of a young woman relative, who, as a student, had spent her gap year as a nanny to a family in America. Things had gone fairly well – though she had not enjoyed having to go to church every Sunday with the two children. But not long before she came home she had asked for an advance on her remaining money so she could book a flight ticket with the cheapest airline. But instead they presented her with a more expensive ticket they had already booked for her with an *American* airline, which they said they had to support. Oh, I think she was unlucky. I think that most American families would not have done that. Most, but not all, whereas you could search the UK – or even all of Europe – from end to end and not find one single family who would have carried patriotism to that extreme.

On a lighter patriotic note there is the notorious film clip of part of a football match between Harvard and Yale Colleges. This was preceded by a lot of razzmatazz with a parade of mini-skirted drum majorettes prancing about and a band playing martial music. However, during play an incident occurred on the pitch causing fighting among the players. The alumni on the platform were appalled. Surely it was only in Europe that there was football hooliganism? And this at Harvard vs. Yale! One of them had a brainwave. Tell the band to strike up the national anthem. It worked! The players immediately stopped brawling and sprang to attention followed by the whole stadium rising to its feet! This film clip has been repeatedly shown not only in this country but in Europe. American visitors are puzzled and offended at Europeans finding this hilarious, as it is what they and indeed every American would do when the national anthem is played anywhere!

But let me end by coming back to what I started with, the American antipathy to any kind of national health system resembling the British NHS. It was this that frustrated President Obama's efforts to reform the notorious system in which Americans spend three times as much per head on private health insurance as we do in taxes for our NHS, and get far less cover for it. Obama wanted to start a government-run scheme for the 20 per cent of Americans who cannot afford health insurance. The insurance companies organised resistance to this on a large scale. We saw, on the TV news, people at meetings shouting down government speakers, and holding up banners saying 'No to Socialism'. Although these were ordinary, not particularly well-off Americans and included black people, the insurance companies had apparently little difficulty in rousing their opposition to a government-run health system. The TV programme had interviews with people who had no health insurance. One was with a man with who had had a leg amputated from diabetes, and was in danger of losing another limb, but was dependent on charities for the drugs that would prevent this. Surely he, of all people, would welcome free health insurance? Not if it was government-run, he said, that's *socialism!* I stared at the TV in disbelief. He seemed to me more foreign than an Outer Mongolian.

There is of course no left-wing politics or press in America. The English couple found that the reason for this and for the fact that both main political parties in America are conservative is that the *people* are conservative. Not just many or even most, but all of them, blacks included. Even militant trade unionists leading strikes are not left-wing.

The couple found that the much-vaunted individualism of American culture is more than offset by their unanimous conservatism on social issues. It was a relief for them to get back to a country where not everybody votes conservative and goes to church on Sundays.

So I think that despite our common language and literature, pop music, Hollywood movies, TV programmes, and, in my own case, a family connection, I, too, would find America a very foreign country.

The Facts of Life

Boys of my generation found out what were called 'the facts of life' somewhat indirectly and haphazardly – from dirty jokes, playground rumours, love scenes in movies. But there was an aspect of it which we learnt about that we found hard to believe. We could easily believe that what girls had between their legs was for males to put their things in to make babies. Most of us had seen it, and not only those of us who had sisters. There was a girl in our class who could be got round with a bar of chocolate to lift up her dress and let you look at her slit. A boy named Sid boasted that he had put his thing in but nobody believed him. One day I got involved in an argument when I claimed that it wasn't the same with older people. Sid was scornful. How do you think they do it then, he sneered. In their sleep, I said. Sid mocked my ignorance and invited the others to join in ridiculing me. But the others did not join in and I realised that I was expressing what they were all – except Sid – having difficulty believing. We could believe it about boys and girls of our age. Indeed, some of us would have liked to try it with the girls in our class if they would have let us. And we could believe it about teenagers. And people in their early twenties. Late twenties? Ye-e-es. Early thirties? Well, maybe. But *forty*? Our parents' ages? Oh God, NO! It would have to be in their sleep. Sid was outraged and took it out on me in various ways for some time afterwards.

A little later there occurred the second memorable event in my education about this fact of life. The war was on and I went to have a secret smoke up a lane with grassy banks. It was nearly dusk. I struck a match to light up and a voice startled me: 'Say, give me a light, bud.' It was an American soldier who, I at first thought, was lying against the bank leaning on his elbows. Then in the half darkness I made out a figure lying under him, a woman. I struck another match and held it to his cigarette. The matchlight illuminated briefly the woman's face. His cape was around them both but her feet were outside his and there was sweat on her brow. I knew by then what that meant. I recognised her. Her husband was away in the Air Force and she was the mother of one of the boys who, like me, had thought that adults only did it in their sleep.

But the third and most memorable occasion dealt finally with my reluctance to face up to reality. It happened at home. My aunt, my mother and two or three other neighbours were chatting over a cup of tea and I was in the parlour. My mother came from a large family in which this aunt was the youngest, being over ten years younger than my mother and very good-looking – indeed, I sometimes brought her image into my mind when I engaged in that solitary act for which I risked going blind. The doors were open so I could hear them talking about a big soprano woman in the church choir who was about to get married to the organist. A right madam. Very stuck up. Would sail past you in the street, her nose in the air. Well, my aunt said with a laugh, she'll have another organ to contend with now. I was shocked. I didn't know that women could talk like that. But the hair really rose on the back of my neck when the others – and my mother – joined in, saying, 'Oh, she will indeed', not with a laugh like my aunt, which would have been shocking enough, but with *grim satisfaction.*

I quietly shut the parlour door and put from my mind for years to come the implications of that grim satisfaction.

Mind Your Language

I emigrated to Australia when I was twenty-one. In a chemical plant where I was working an English immigrant was told to do something by the foreman, who, a little later, became angry at it not being done. 'I told you to do it *presently*,' the foreman said. I came to the man's assistance, explaining that in England 'presently' means *soon, in a little while*, whereas in Australia it means *immediately, right now*, which, I might have further explained, was keeping the meaning it had for Captain Cook and the original settlers, or indeed Shakespeare. 'Effing Poms!' the foreman said to me contemptuously, knowing he could say that to me, being Irish, since this derogatory term applies only to the English. This was a fact which a group of German-speaking immigrants I worked with were grateful to me for explaining because it was something about their new country that was puzzling them. Not all the British immigrants, I worked out them telling each other delightedly, catching the words *Pommy bastard* and *Englischer Einwanderer*.

I have never seen a satisfactory explanation of the origin of the derogatory Australian term *Poms* for English immigrants. Linking it to the name of the Pomeranian breed of dog does not quite fit. Irish immigrants getting their own back? Or perhaps also the marginalised Welsh and Scots?

Afrikaans-speaking South Africans encounter even more embarrassing misunderstandings if they visit the Netherlands and find their seventeenth-century Dutch being laughed at. The shoe can be on the other foot, however, when it comes to the – sometimes – comic resemblances between Dutch and English. Both countries are monarchies with horse guards stationed at the palaces and riding in procession at ceremonial occasions. Some years ago it was thought that it would be a good idea for the two countries to swap some horse guards. These are paraded in the morning for inspection just like the foot guards. After inspection the order is given 'Mount the horses'. The English horse guards came back from the Netherlands and said that there the order was 'Clamber oop de beasties'.

The Australian usage of the word 'pub' can also be confusing. It does not mean a drinking establishment, which in Australia is a 'bar'. There a pub is a 'hotel'. Consequently there are non-alcoholic *temperance* pubs! But, at the time of the first settlements in Australia a drinking establishment in England was called a 'tavern', so why was that term not taken to Australia? And in England why – and when – did tavern become *public house*? And why was its abbreviation pub taken to Australia as *hotel*?

When the British and American armies invaded Europe in 1944 they, of course, encountered children. Some soldiers thought it would be funny to teach the French children our swear words and obscenities but not their meanings. This resulted in other soldiers – and English-speaking French people, not to mention the parents of the children – being appalled at hearing, for example, a sweet little girl or an angelic-looking little boy, proudly showing off their English by loudly effing and blinding.

Then there are the differences between American English and our own. Telling an American that you'll give them a ring would puzzle them as to why you wanted to give them something to put on their finger. In America you give them a call. There are many other examples of things being named differently such as faucet for tap or the euphemism washroom for toilet. However these cause little real embarrassment. For that the prize has to go to the word that every American posted to the American Embassy in London is warned about. The story is often told of the newly arrived junior diplomat, who, at an embassy function, thought the guests would be amused by his account of a cocktail party at 10 Downing Street when he had unfortunately stumbled against Mrs Thatcher and, as he put it, 'accidentally patted her on her fanny' – ha, ha. He could not understand the sudden silence, the mass intake of breath, the shocked gasps until he was hustled to one side and accused of not having read or paid attention to the instructions about different meanings for the same words in the two cultures of which *fanny* was *Number One.* Whereas in America it is simply a mildly vulgar word for *backside*, as in *he* slipped and fell on his *fanny*, on this side of the Atlantic it differs from that meaning to a degree which, in the words of the American writer Damon (*Guys and Dolls*) Runyon, is more than somewhat.

Borrowing from other languages can be confusing or plain wrong. Take, for instance, the English word affair. My wife, while working in France, was shocked to be told by a woman that she was having an annoying *affaire*, assuming it meant the same as in English, i.e. having an (adulterous) affair, whereas in French affaire means only the other meaning of the English word affair, i.e. event, business, happening. Confused?

I did the old school certificate in Spanish, which I have now almost completely forgotten. However, if I were to read aloud from a Spanish book or newspaper to Spanish people they would easily understand what I was reading even though I would not. That is because Spanish is a phonetic language – that is, the same group of letters in different words is pronounced in exactly the same way. Compare that with English. Why do the words 'chalk' and 'hawk' have the same sound as do 'folk' and 'yoke'? What is the *p* doing in 'psychology' or 'psalm'? The spelling in English is a joke, though it is not funny to bewildered foreigners trying to learn it.

Then there is our grammar, which foreigners consider even more of a joke. In French, for instance, if a sentence is grammatical it will not be bad French. But in English the connection between good English and good grammar is virtually non-existent. As has been often remarked, it is perfectly possible to compose a sentence in English that is perfectly grammatical but perfectly awful. English that sounds or reads well is composed only by people who care deeply for the language. Yet, paradoxically, the very disorderliness of English may be part of the reason why some passages of English are among the most beautiful in any language. Although I have been long an atheist, I am not entirely regretful of my upbringing in the church-going Protestant community of Northern Ireland where I attended Sunday school. I can still quote from the Bible: 'Though I speak with the tongues of men and of angels and have not charity I am become as sounding brass or a tinkling symbol…' I could go on… That is as fine a piece of English as anything in Shakespeare. It is of course from the Authorised or King James version in which 'existing translations were diligently compared and revised'. They did more comparing than revising and a great deal of it is from the translation by William Tyndale who was burnt at the stake for blasphemy because Latin was the only language permitted by the church for the Bible.

Some years ago the Anglican Church tried to introduce a new English translation to replace the King James version. This was greeted – quite rightly – by a chorus of outrage from all sides, so that the Church commented acidly on the bizarre spectacle of Bible-loving atheists like Michael Foot being bedfellows with Gospel Hall evangelists in leaping to the defence of the King James version!

I have a stepdaughter who is half Spanish and was for a time an agency Spanish interpreter at international conferences. She told me about the problem faced by German interpreters. Germans put the verb at the end of sentences. That last sentence in German would go: 'The Germans at the end sentences the verbs put'. Since verbs are the most important words in sentences the German interpreter has to wait for the end of a sentence, to begin interpreting it and, if it is a long sentence, will have to rush to catch up. So German speakers were asked to keep their sentences as short as possible to assist the interpreter. There is a button on an interpreter's microphone to press if they want to cough or sneeze. But the German interpreter in the next glass booth to my stepdaughter was pressing it for a different reason. It was to shout: 'Give me a verb, you Kraut windbag!'

The term 'pidgin English' comes from a Chinese term meaning language for trading and was widely used in Victorian times throughout Asia. It even achieved the ultimate in being recognised as a language in its own right when a Bible translation into pidgin English was commissioned by the British and Foreign Bible Society. The passage '. . . and Jesus went forth among the multitudes' is rendered '. . . Him big boss fella he go walk about'. Pidgin is a very economical language. There is no past tense and vocabulary is greatly reduced by use of the word 'belong'. Thus a bird's wing is *hand belong bird* and a spouse or partner is *woman belong man* or vice versa. Papua New Guinea uses pidgin as an official language because it is so mountainous that the tribes on different sides of a mountain do not speak the same language. On a state visit by the Duke of Edinburgh he heard himself being introduced to the Papuan parliament by the Speaker as 'him big fella belong missy Queen'.

Our English language is, of course continually evolving; some of the changes are an improvement, others not. It is good that we have got rid of the nonsense that prohibited ending a phrase or sentence with a preposition. Schoolboys were made to rewrite 'the room I came out of' as 'the room out of which I came'. Editors would 'correct' the best authors. Even the great Winston Churchill was not allowed to get away with it. As he said of this in his memoirs, 'up with which they would not put'. On the other hand, there are changes to the meanings of words which are bad, even crass. Why has the word 'impact', which used to be used about a crash or a blow, come to replace the words *effect* and *affect* so that we now read about 'the impact of the tax changes on business', or, even worse, 'The school plans are impacting on the young.' Then there is pompous jargon replacing plain English. We have come a long way since a spade became 'an agricultural implement'. Today we have employees called 'human resources', deaths and injuries to civilians in war called 'collateral damage', and, God help us, what authors of fiction do called 'creative writing', so as to use it as a pompous title for jobs at universities – 'Professor of Creative Writing'.

An American couple in Taiwan employed a Chinese nanny for their small child. They discovered that at the same time as it was learning to talk English from them it was also learning to speak good Chinese from just hearing it spoken by the nanny and her friends and never for a moment confused the two languages. They thought they had a genius on their hands but were disappointed to be told that all children can do that. This was demonstrated during the boom years of immigration into the USA. Thus, adult Italians too poor to take English lessons spoke broken English for the rest of their lives – 'da fish a da chip and da ice a da cream' – but not Italian children who picked up perfect English from simply hearing it spoken around them. But why should this cause surprise? We ourselves as very young children learn to speak without any formal instruction. This involves a mental process that is still not understood. After all, learning a language consists of much more than learning the names of things: Dada, chair, you, me and so on. It means learning the rules of grammar. Children at school find the definition of complex rules of grammar difficult to understand – subject, object, past tense, future conditional, adverbial subclause and so on – even though they have been applying the rules perfectly accurately before they came to school. Simply from hearing people speak, children work out the complex rules of grammar without any instruction. *All* children, including the not so bright, and even the mentally impaired. This ability has resulted in some experts advancing the theory that language learning in the very young uses a part of the brain not connected with intelligence and created during evolution for that sole purpose but which gradually atrophies as children grow older, until in adults it has disappeared completely.

Next time you hear a young pre-school child speak a perfectly grammatical sentence just marvel at the wonder of it.

Privacy

Like many other things we take for granted, privacy is, historically, a comparatively recent luxury. What could be more private than the most pressing bodily function – using the loo. Yet in Roman public lavatories there were no cubicles. Men chatted to each other while emptying their bowels. It was before the invention of paper and the piece of sponge on the end of a stick with which they wiped their bottoms was ... communal.

By the Middle Ages some big houses had a little cubicle perched over a moat or stream. So you would think privacy would improve from then on. Well, no. In a French chateau that had been built in the Middle Ages but refurbished in the eighteenth century the shape of a bedroom looked odd to the present-day national custodians. Taking away the layers of paint and paper they discovered a covered-up cubicle which had undoubtedly been a lavatory for which the eighteenth-century refurbishers no longer had a use. Why not? Because, while the eighteenth century may have been the Age of Enlightenment, it was also the age of the chamber pot.

Before the French Revolution there would have been seen every morning a procession coming from the palace of Versailles. It was of chambermaids bearing chamber pots to empty onto the royal midden. Nor would the chamber pots have come only from the bedrooms. How do you suppose they provided for the attendees of a great function or glittering ball? Well, a servant in a distinctive livery would be stationed at the door of a large room in which the only furniture would be – yes, – chamber pots. Chamber pots were everywhere at one time. On a recent episode of *Antiques Roadshow* on TV, the owner was puzzled by a strange compartment in an old desk. It was for a chamber pot.

In stately homes open to the public, visitors cannot have failed to notice that, to get from one end of the building to another, you have to go through all the rooms. There were no corridors. The corridor is a late architectural innovation. Guests would get to their bedrooms by going through other guests' bedrooms, and when in them they would be liable to have other people going through them unannounced, including maids bearing things to and from other bedrooms – such as chamber pots. It is likely that the curtain around the four-poster bed provided the only privacy that guests would ever know – apart from screens to use the chamber pot. Dressing and undressing was not only done in front of the servants but was done with the assistance of the servants.

Of course, the poor never had any kind of privacy but there is no reason to suppose that they would not have liked to have it, so why did the wealthy in their great houses not provide themselves with a room – a study, an office, whatever – having a door that could be firmly shut, requiring anyone wishing to enter to knock and wait for a called-out permission to be allowed in? Such a room only became possible after the architectural innovation of the corridor. We take the need for privacy so much for granted that it is difficult to understand why even the richest of our comparatively recent forebears chose to live most of their lives in public. Samuel Pepys, now remembered only for his diary but who in fact was virtually the founder of a standing British navy (before Pepys, ships had been assembled and crews found only when a war broke out), once consulted with the king in his bedroom. This was crowded with courtiers, even though the king was not only in bed but had Nell Gwyn – his current mistress – in bed beside him.

When the queen or indeed the wives of the nobility gave birth, they were not attended only by midwives. The bedroom would be crowded with spectators, not only to witness the authenticity of the birth to protect the inheritance (because of the fear of changelings being smuggled in), but also because it was not considered a very private event.

Public executions were stopped only as late as the mid-nineteenth century. To the crowds who flocked to watch them the idea of a secluded room for the hanging attended only by the hangman and two or three prison warders would have seemed very peculiar.

Why was our need for privacy so late in arriving and why did it develop when it did?

We are so used to scattered farms and cottages in the countryside that we need to be reminded that there were times when farm workers lived in villages from which they went out to work the land every day, as they still do in France. So even when the population of this country was a fraction of what it is today, it was not only in cities but in the countryside that people were huddled together and everybody knew everything about everybody else. Was the habit of living at close quarters with each other so long established that it was difficult to break? Was it the Industrial Revolution that broke it, especially after the coming of the railways? Men who had lived and died within ten miles of their birthplace could now travel to the other end of the country to find work, and finding not only work but work among strangers who did not know all about them – finding, in other words, the luxury of privacy, the appreciation of which probably spread rapidly. The arrival of the railway age and the corridor in houses is probably not a coincidence.

But even with the arrival of the corridor and the

consequent 'privatising' of some rooms, the upper classes still have to put up with much less privacy than the rest of us because of the constant presence of servants from which only the man can briefly escape into his study – though not his wife or children. The phrase *not in front of the servants* must still apply and must still inhibit much upper-class family life. The privacy which we ordinary people take for granted is probably the one – if the only – thing in our lives that the upper classes envy.

Whom the Gods Love Die Young

Hurricane Higgins

World champion snooker player Alex 'Hurricane' Higgins has just died - July 2010 - at the age of sixty. Tributes have been paid on TV and in the national papers to the big part he played in promoting snooker from a game originally played only in snooker halls and public houses to a game played on TV watched by millions of viewers, most of whom have never played snooker and never would play it, yet became, like me, such keen regular viewers that we have no difficulty understanding the commentary when they refer to the positions of the balls. '... He'll need to come off the left-side cushion ... That was not a good cannon ... If he misses again it will be a free ball ... can only play a safety shot ... needs both the brown and the green ...'

Higgins was from working-class backstreet Belfast. He got his nickname from the speed with which he could pocket balls after only the briefest survey of the table, sometimes little more than a glance. During his career snooker not only attracted huge TV viewing figures but snooker halls were filled with big paying audiences to watch tournaments, with players earning big money. Higgins became a millionaire.

His high point came when he won the world championship and we saw him calling his wife and their baby out from the audience to hug them, so overcome with emotion that he was in tears. That TV moment was replayed as we watched his huge funeral in Belfast. But things thereafter went downhill. He was still for a time a big TV performer, but his bad behaviour became notorious. We saw him shouting abuse at a referee and headbutting the sponsor of a tournament, drawing blood above his eye. He failed to turn up for matches. He acquired three addictions: gambling, booze and chain-smoking (TV snooker was sponsored by a big cigarette manufacturer). The first got rid of his money. It is not clear which of the other two killed him first. His wife divorced him.

He eventually returned to Belfast to live his last years, his gaunt wasted face a familiar sight in its snooker halls and public houses. What sadder last years could there be for a one-time millionaire world champion than playing for beer money at public-house snooker tables in his native city and dying alone in his backstreet house, his body not discovered for three days.

Wordsworth

At school, along with Shakespeare, we got quite a big dose of Wordsworth. I still remember some of it:

I wandered lonely as a cloud
That floats on high o'er vales and hills,
When all at once I saw a crowd
A host of golden daffodils.

He was a friend of Hazlitt and Coleridge with whom he collaborated in the writing of the *Lyrical Ballads* when he was in his twenties. He went on to write many more poems and was eventually made Poet Laureate in late middle age. It is thought that this honour was awarded as much for his support for the government as for his poetry. He opposed both reform bills aimed at addressing the worst features of early-nineteenth-century society – the kind famously exposed by Charles Dickens and others: the workhouse, pocket borough elections, child labour and so on.

So could this crabbed old reactionary have any possible connection with the young man whose passion for social justice took him to France at the outbreak of the French Revolution where he fell in love and fathered a child in an affair celebrated in a poem, and wrote the words quoted ever since by those campaigning against great wrongs:

Bliss was it in that dawn to be alive,
And to be young was very heaven!

A young man by the name of William Wordsworth. The same. The very same.

The Merry Monarch

He was the most handsome Prince in Christendom. He was a superb horseman, not only in the chase but in jousting tournaments. He held his own with the best at archery. He could take on champion wrestlers. He spoke fluent French. He wrote religious dissertations in Latin that was up to the standard of churchmen. He was an accomplished musician and composed choral pieces still occasionally sung by choirs to this day. He wrote a love poem quoted by James Joyce.

So who was this paragon of all the princely virtues, whose reign would surely usher in a golden age of monarchy? He was Henry the Eighth, of the six unfortunate wives, who became so gross that a crane was needed to winch him into the saddle of his horse, and was described by

Charles Dickens as a blot of blood and grease upon the page of English history.

Marie Antoinette

In 1770 a daughter of the Holy Roman Emperor Francis I left her beloved Vienna for Paris at the age of fifteen to become the bride of the Dauphin, heir to the throne of France, of which she would become queen.

So what was her adopted country like at the time of her arrival? Voltaire was being acclaimed as a great thinker. Lavoisier had isolated and identified oxygen as a basic element and so founded the science of chemistry, getting rid of the alchemists searching for the philosopher's stone or the secret of turning lead into gold. Montgolfier went up into the sky in his hot air balloon to cheering crowds to begin the conquest of space. Paris was leading the world in what was being called the 'Age of Enlightenment'.

But Paris was not France. Under this brilliant veneer, most of the population of what was still a feudal kingdom – twenty million of them – lived hard toil-worn lives, sometimes starving. Across the Channel in England there had once been similar conditions, which had led to Wat Tyler's Peasants' Revolt in the fifteenth century which nearly seized London with its slogan: 'When Adam walked and Eve span who was then a gentleman'. But although the revolt was brutally crushed, the English nobility was astute enough to realise that it would have to somewhat loosen its grip, that it would have to give up some of its privileges in order to hold on to most of them. This pattern of gradually giving way a little at a time was still continuing in England in the late eighteenth century but had not even started in France. The nobility – *la noblesse* – were blind and deaf to the crying need for them to change. It is true that the most bizarre of their privileges, such as the right to first night with the newly married brides of their tenants, was no longer enforced. But they were the frills on the main privilege: they and the Church did not pay any taxes. By the 1780s France was so hard up that half the navy could not put to sea because there was no money to repair the ships.

The French Revolution was an eruption waiting to happen. Yet it began not with an uprising from the oppressed poor but with howls of outrage from the nobility at the effrontery of being asked to pay some taxes. They found in Marie Antoinette a champion of their resistance to reform. Her influence on King Louis, an absolute monarch, but by no means a tyrant, was to stop him bringing about any change to what she was used to. It was to cost her dear.

When the violence of the Revolution had burnt the chateaux of the nobility and guillotined those of them who did not flee the country, it put King Louis on trial and guillotined him, too, throwing Marie Antoinette into a common prison. When they put her on trial six months later there is some evidence that even Robespierre, architect of the Reign of Terror as it is called, wanted to spare her life and send her into exile, but too much was remembered against her. Her extravagance. Her jewels. The story that had swept the country how, when thousands of hungry women had marched to the palace at Versailles crying 'Give us bread!', she was reported to have said, 'Let them eat cake', which, while almost certainly untrue, unfortunately fitted her other attitudes and behaviour.

So, on 16 October 1793, one of the tumbrels carrying the condemned to the place of execution had in it Marie Antoinette, grey-haired and prematurely aged, bearing herself with great dignity, her only slight display of emotion when the tumbrel passed what had been the Tuileries Palace and her head turned towards it. She must have been remembering when she had come to it as the child-woman whose beauty was the adornment of the court in which the most handsome men in France had vied for the honour of kissing her hand. Remembering, too, a very different vehicle she had been carried in through these same streets as a beautiful young queen – her royal coach, also, like the tumbrel, accompanied by cavalry, but not, as now, to protect her from the jeering mobs shouting '*Vive la Republique*', but from their enthusiastic affection, as they shouted, '*Vive la reine*'.

Elvis

People who are old enough to remember the years when pop songs sold millions of records may also be ashamed to admit that they have forgotten the names of the singers that they themselves once hailed as idols. Who now remembers the likes of Johnny Ray? Johnny *who*? I hear you ask. Yet they once filled concert halls with adoring fans. Hordes of girls rose screaming from their seats at the sight of their gyrations on stage, some of them fainting and having to be carried out by the Red Cross. The fame of only a few has survived, such as Bing Crosby and Frank Sinatra, and even then much diminished. But there is one who achieved what probably no other singer of any kind has ever done – to still be known the world over by his first name alone – Elvis.

Elvis Presley was born and reared in the state of Mississippi in the American deep south into a family that belonged to a Pentecostal church characterised by loud rhythmic feet-tramping gospel hymn-singing that he loved for the rest of his life. Indeed, it was his singing in church that first attracted attention and got him on the air, first from his local radio station, then from the bigger one in Memphis and then into other states of the South before being taken up by a record company. He was famous by the age of twenty for rock and roll songs that are still well known – *Hound Dog, Love Me Tender, All Shook Up*. In the year 1958 he earned a million dollars from his records – that would be ten million in today's money. He was THE KING.

Yet his title of 'King' was not entirely due to his position at the top of pop music. He built himself a huge mansion named Graceland, after his mother Grace, with whom he had such a lifelong close relationship (for the rest of his life he mourned her early death at the age of thirty-seven), that rumours have been spread about possible incest, almost certainly untrue. But he installed her in Graceland along with many other relatives and friends – on full board and lodging of course – from whom he expected a deference bordering on obeisance. He was highly competitive and they had to let him win at everything. At five-a-side football, for instance, he had to be allowed to score the winning goal. At one game of cards his wife's foot was pressed under the table to warn her she was in danger of winning! That cards anecdote could have come straight from the memoirs of a courtier at the palace of Versailles before the French Revolution.

He could do nothing in moderation. When his teenage daughter took up horse riding he took it up, too. So his whole household had to learn to ride, for which he bought a ranch to stable the horses – all thoroughbreds. Then there was the motor-bike phase and they were all roaring through the countryside on motor-bikes to the complaints of neighbours. He was semi-nocturnal and would rouse forty of his 'best friends' from their beds in the early hours to go in a cavalcade of cars to a restaurant in Memphis which had to open specially. Despite his vast earnings, there was one year he managed to live beyond his income.

He not only became an addict to prescription drugs that

he tossed into his mouth like popcorn, he made his love of food almost an addiction in itself. His flamboyant clothes had to be designed to disguise his increasing stoutness at his concerts. It is unclear which addiction, drugs or food – especially the fatty foods he gorged on – did more to kill him.

My wife was in a car park in London when, in 1977, a man came into it weeping and calling out 'Elvis is dead'. Yet surely the Elvis he and millions more were grieving for was not that sick and bloated man of forty-two, but the young Greek-god-like singer of 'Ain't Nothin' But a Hound Dog', so handsome that a word had been used to describe him never used about even the most glamorous of male Hollywood heart-throbs – *beautiful.* When the American government put his handsome young face on a postage stamp it had only one word on it – ELVIS.

Bonny Prince Charlie

The Stewart royal dynasty is not one proudly celebrated in English history. It started with James the First who had been James the Sixth of Scotland, brought to the English throne when Queen Elizabeth, the great virgin queen, died without an heir. Although a very learned man whose name appears on the great Authorised Version of the Bible, his table manners were such that he was mocked as 'Slabbering Jamie'. His son, Charles the First, tried to impose 'the divine right of kings' to be absolute rulers and had his head chopped off for trying to suppress Parliament.

Charles's son, Charles the Second, is remembered more for having Nell Gwyn as one of his many mistresses than for anything else. His brother, who became James the Second, tried to restore the Catholic religion and was chased out of England into Ireland by his daughter's husband, William of Orange, who defeated him at the Battle of the Boyne and chased him into France where he became the grandfather of Charles, known firstly as 'the Young Pretender' from his claim to the English throne, but later, and more famously, as 'Bonny Prince Charlie'.

How close that claim came to being realised is disputed by historians. The French army that would have supported his first attempt by invading Kent was scattered by a terrible storm. A year or so later he tried again but without French help, landing in the Hebrides with only a few followers. However, the clans rallied to his cause, and he entered Edinburgh in triumph, setting up a royal court at Holyrood. It is said that the ladies swooned over him, he was so handsome. His army defeated the English army at the Battle of Prestonpans and he pressed on into England, reaching as far as Derby. All England was thrown into a panic and there is a famous painting by Hogarth of a hastily assembled English regiment mustering in Finchley Road, London, to defend the capital. But the panic was needless. The invasion of England did not have the popular support it had had in Scotland. Disagreements broke out in Charles's army whether to go on or go back and there were some desertions. It was decided to withdraw. The withdrawal became a retreat. In Scotland came the defeat at Culloden – in which the clan Campbell fought on the side of the English – which not only ended the possibility of a Stewart restoration but brought about the crushing of the clans. Thereafter 'Scottishness' became almost a quaint display of picturesque customs – playing the bagpipes, toasting the haggis, tossing the caber, Rabbie Burns, Hogmanay, Auld Lang Syne . . . Even the kilt was a Victorian invention – the Highlanders had worn trews.

The romantic story of Prince Charles's flight through the heather disguised as a woman helped by Flora Macdonald has been celebrated not only in print but in film. He got back to France where he was put up for a time at the court of King Louis, taking solace in drink and women, but was a political embarrassment to French foreign policy and he was put up for a time around the courts of Europe, ending up in Florence where he married a countess and lived till nearly seventy. But when the Scots sang ‘Will he no come back again’, it was not that forgotten figure they meant but the earlier one in another song: ‘Carry the lad that is born to be King / Over the sea to Skye’. Bonny Prince Charlie.

The Industrial Revolution

I

We are often told that we live in a time of great change, as indeed we do. Package holidays spent seeing the Great Wall of China. Mobile phones that are also cameras. The Internet. And much more. Yet there was a time when people's lives were changed to a degree probably greater than what is happening today. The time of the Industrial Revolution.

The invention of the steam locomotive, and with it the coming of the railways, are often thought of as the Industrial Revolution itself. This is understandable. A country in which the once predominantly rural population lived out their lives within ten miles of their birthplace, and long journeys by stagecoach could involve overnight stops, was transformed by the railways into one in which men could seek work hundreds of miles away by making journeys that took only hours.

But the invention of the steam engine that brought about the Industrial Revolution happened nearly forty years before its adaptation in Stevenson's *Rocket* of 1829 – which pulled the first train. The story of James Watt being inspired to invent the steam engine by watching boiling water push up the lid of a kettle is a myth told to schoolchildren. Newcomen's atmospheric engine was already pumping water out of the mines in the 1750s. But it was purely a pump whose piston worked only up and down, steam driving it down and then cold water on the cylinder condensing the steam and creating a vacuum that sucked it up again from the pressure of the atmosphere. Watt, as well as designing valves to let the steam in and out of the cylinder, made the piston drive a wheel, creating *rotary* motion, so that it could be used for other purposes besides pumping. Richard Trevithick actually installed one in a coach in 1803 that ran in London at nine miles an hour, anticipating railways, but their first use was of course in mills. Mills that had previously been powered by water wheels had steam engines installed in them as early as 1790.

When I first visited Lancashire I was struck by the similarity of the landscape to that in Northern Ireland where I grew up – mill chimneys all around. In my first job in a mill after leaving school, a part of the office used by the directors was still called by its eighteenth-century name 'The Counting House', and above its entrance was the date 1793. In a glass case was a cutting from a newspaper of that time describing the transporting of a steam engine and boiler from the docks on a huge specially-made cart with many wheels pulled by a team of horses.

That mill became the biggest thread mill in the world, just as, in Belfast, the small shipyard that started up at about the same time became the biggest in the world and built the *Titanic*. Around the mill I remember streets of small two-up two-down houses that were condemned as slums and pulled down after the Second World War. They had been built by the mill owners for the workers who had streamed in from the countryside. But they should be compared not with what replaced them but with what the previously agricultural workers had left behind: thatched cottages that look so picturesque on postcards but were in fact insanitary hovels to which water had to be fetched from wells up to half a mile away and lavatories that were either a hole in the ground outside or a bucket inside. Those two-up two-down houses in fact represented an enormous improvement in the conditions of the common people: they had an inside water tap and outside in a little yard a flush lavatory. Indeed, the Industrial Revolution virtually created what became known as the working class. For all the smoke and the grime and the poverty, given the choice between the age of the mills and factories and what preceded it, nobody in their right mind in the working class would have gone back to the serfdom of agriculture.

Of course the working class did have its own tiers. The phrase 'upper working class' no longer has much meaning but it did once, when it meant rather more than distinguishing the skilled from the unskilled. It meant people like my father, a shoemaker, one of my uncles, a railway engine driver, and another who was in charge of a railway signal cabin. Carpenters. Bricklayers. Tailors. Machinists. Lathe turners.

The last named – the men who could work in steel to a thousandth of an inch – epitomised what made Britain 'the workshop of the world'. There is no more fitting example of their craft than the most famous clock in the world, Big Ben. Its massive machinery is so precisely made that its timekeeping can be corrected by a penny coin slid a very little way forwards or backwards on a slim steel bar.

II

There are two countries to which the term '*Industrial Revolution*' is now applied: India and China. In the India of saris and paddy fields that was once 'the white man's burden', over half of the cars on its streets and roads will today have been manufactured in India itself; the quality of its university degrees in engineering is such as to create a shortage of them in India from so many engineering graduates being lured to the US by American engineering companies. China is building so many power stations and factories that it is the chief polluter of the atmosphere. So does this mean that the changes taking place in China and India are following the same route once taken by the industrial revolutions in nineteenth-century Europe?

At first glance it would certainly seem so. A recent TV programme showed a main street in Shanghai and the scene would have been similar in Mumbai in India. Well-dressed people going in and out of shops and department stores identical to those of London's Oxford Street; traffic congestion in which there may well be more new cars than in Central London. The middle classes of India and China have undoubtedly done well out of their industrial revolutions.

So what happened to the people who, just as in Europe at industrialisation, fled from poverty in the countryside into the cities, especially in China after the Communist Party allowed capitalism to release the peasants from the bondage of the state farms? Did they get two-up two-down houses with an inside water tap and a flush lavatory in the yard? No. Shanty towns of overcrowded corrugated-tin dwellings lacking the most basic amenities, some with an open sewer running down the main street. The industrial revolutions in China and India have not done what happened in Europe – produced a reasonably well-housed *working class.* Indeed, the Chinese government is worried that the gap between the burgeoning middle class and the 'underclass' is actually widening. It is not only in India and China that the new industrial revolutions are happening; Brazil is now an emerging world power as a major oil producer. But it is the same story as in Mumbai or Shanghai. Glittering office blocks and well-dressed people patronising the shopping arcades of Rio de Janeiro. Yet on the outskirts are packed shanty towns lacking basic amenities.

The nineteenth-century mill owners, hard-faced though

they were, nevertheless provided their exploited and underpaid workers with two-up two-down houses that had an inside water tap and a flush lavatory, and so we avoided the violent social upheavals - even if sometimes only just - of the French and Russian Revolutions.

Let us hope that the present industrial revolutions in China, India and South America do not engulf us all in catastrophe.

Aspects of Sex

Sailors in Nelson's time were allowed in port to bring women aboard to spend the night with them in their hammocks. The wake up call by the bosun was 'Show a leg' – that is, a woman's leg. Those who did so were allowed to get up an hour later. Mothers still use it to call their children in the mornings without knowing where it came from.

*

Catching venereal disease was a punishable offence in both the British and American armies in the Second World War since it made a soldier unfit for duty. But the policies to prevent it differed somewhat. In American bases there was a big dish in the canteen full of condoms from which the soldiers helped themselves. British soldiers had to apply for them to the medical officer who would, of course, know from their papers whether they were married or single. Consequently the per capita infection rate in the British army was five times that of the American.

*

The age of consent in this country is sixteen. A man having sex with a girl under that age is committing a criminal offence. In some other countries the age is as low as twelve, which at first sight seems wrong. But then consider the case of parents with a daughter aged fifteen years and eleven months and a youth of eighteen whom the parents want prosecuted. Either the police would regard it as a waste of police time or a court would throw it out. But in countries with a lower age of consent such cases would always be prosecuted. It is perhaps better to have a law that is always enforced rather than a law whose enforcement is discretionary.

*

Does size matter? Teenage boys steal surreptitious glances at their neighbours using the urinals and are not reassured by subsequently consulting the ruler or tape measure. Perhaps they should be told that the size of the flaccid penis is no guide to its size when erect. Penises that are small when flaccid may swell on arousal to even bigger size than larger ones. Whether it matters to women involves the controversy over the vaginal orgasm. A woman's clitoris is sited close to the vaginal entrance and hence can be stimulated to orgasm by any size of penis. It would be different with the vagina, but then many doubt whether there is such a thing as vaginal orgasm.

*

When I was twelve I once went to a party given by our new church curate to mark our confirmation – the church ceremony officiated by the bishop which celebrates boys and girls leaving childhood behind. He was a very modern curate who smoked. He announced at the party that he believed the boys and girls should get to know each other. He organised kissing games which went down so well that we wanted to keep it going at the end of the party and chased the girls through the streets on the way home. Some of the girls did not run as hard as the others. I got one up against a yard door in an alleyway. The door opened suddenly and we fell in a heap. A woman looked at us scrambling to our feet and said, 'In the name of God, you're early at it!'

*

A radio speaker once got into trouble for saying that it was actually not easy to get pregnant. It was felt that this sent the wrong message to teenagers. It is certainly true that conception can occur from a one-off act of intercourse, but this does not contradict the findings of a study by an American university which interviewed many couples with children. It came up with the finding that it takes, on average, seventy acts of sexual intercourse between couples of child-bearing age to bring about conception. Every GP will have had visits from worried young couples trying to conceive. Asked how long they have been trying and if they reply about four months, they will be surprised to learn that this is quite common. A survey of birth certificates from the days when most births occurred within marriage showed how few occurred nine months from the wedding day.

*

At one time the Catholic Church had such power in Ireland that condoms were not only unavailable but illegal. They were, of course, available in British Northern Ireland. At customs posts on the border, luggage could be searched and finding condoms could result in prosecution. But customs posts were sited only on main roads and so it was easy for enterprising traders to bring in condoms in large quantities. No couple in Ireland had any difficulty obtaining them. And obtained they certainly were. Even during the years of the bigot premier de Valéra who boasted of having made Ireland the most Catholic country in the world, the Irish birth rate was no different from that of the UK, the meaning of which is obvious. Yet every attempt in Ireland until recent times to change the law was successfully resisted by the Catholic Church preaching against the evil of contraception. The Catholic Church succeeded in turning Ireland into a nation of hypocrites who publicly supported the Church's ban on contraception while privately practising it in their bedrooms.

*

The word 'propaganda' actually comes from the Catholic Church where it refers to teaching or guidance on doctrine. Against de Valéra's boast that he had made Ireland and its institutions the most Catholic in the world must be set the awkward fact – not publicised by the Irish hierarchy – that the Irish Catholic Church is deemed by the Vatican to be 'in need of propaganda'. That is because of the Irish excessive veneration of the Virgin Mary or, to give this deviation from doctrine its religious term, *Mariolatry.* Mary is, of course, revered by Catholics everywhere, but in Ireland this is taken to an extreme. This carries just a slight whiff of heresy, though it would be inadvisable to tell that to an Irish Catholic. The effect this Mariolatry has on the general Irish population goes beyond the excessive appearance of the picture of Mary on parlour walls in Ireland. It also results in the elevation of the status of the mother in Ireland. The holy Irish mother. There are, or used to be, grown men in Ireland who could never come to terms with the fact that their mothers could possibly have engaged in sexual intercourse to bring them into the world. Some of them took to drink, others remained bachelors – still on their mothers' hands at the age of forty – or, if not, were, according to the testimony of their partners, poor performers in the bedroom.

*

In the tragic-comic film *Midnight Cowboy* a young Texan shoeshine man with a cough from the polish has an improbable close friend – a more stereotypical Texan, tall and gangling with tooled leather boots. This friend is aware of his shortcomings as regards jobs but feels this is more than made up for by another more important quality. 'I sure am one hell of a stud,' he claims. So his shoeshine mate proposes to exploit this great gift by them going to New York and hiring out the services of the great stud to bored unsatisfied housewives. There is a wonderful brief scene in the film of the shoeshine man waiting outside the door of a hotel room. The door opens and a woman's bare arm appears holding a tooled leather boot, which she then throws out contemptuously. The great stud had not been able to rise to the occasion. But then this can happen – and indeed has happened – to most men whether they would admit it or not. There is, however, a rare genre of males who are immune. The word 'gigolo' is widely misunderstood to mean simply a successful womaniser, a man who has a way with the ladies. But many were surprised to learn its real meaning in an interesting TV programme a few years ago. An elderly, ordinary-looking Italian contemptuously dismissed the right of such men to be called gigolos. He was proud of having been a *true* gigolo, *a man with a gift from God.* Such a God-gifted man can perform sexually with any woman, any looks, any age, any time. This gift had enabled him to live a life of luxury. He had been put up at all the top world hotels – the London Ritz, the Paris Ritz, the New York Waldorf Astoria. He had sailed in the state rooms of ocean liners like the *Queen Mary* and the *Normandie*. He had lived on the Riviera and on Palm Beach. That was what it meant to be a true gigolo.

*

In the Vatican library there are rare old books allowed to be seen only by those given special permission for good reason such as scholarship or research. There are many books on the sex act, which might be thought surprising as the authors were supposedly celibate churchmen. Nevertheless, they are not only detailed and compendious but as accurate as those of today. Some of them are about cases of non-consummation of marriage, whether wilful or arising from impotence. These cases could challenge inheritance rights to estates or titles. The Church disliked such cases because they involved a form of semi-public testing which 'excited the lewdness of the multitude'. The religious authorities employed wives of mature years to conduct the tests:

> ... the three wives will testify to the court that the husband was or was not able in their presence to have full coitus with the wife without unnatural acts or potions ... no premature exterior ejaculation ... semen to depth of at least one finger joint ... second attempt allowed within five hours ... bread and wine but no garlic ... children to be declared bastards without inheritance ... cases requiring fine judgement to be referred to Rome...

The last impotence case was in the seventeenth century and involved a count. He was a notorious rake and was therefore understandably incensed when rumours began to circulate that his reputation was all a front and that he was in fact impotent. He himself demanded to take the test. The Church tried to talk him out of it. Even the most virile men might be put off by having to ... in front of examiners... But he was adamant. How dare they! Him! A five-times-a-night man! Lay it on! He invited a crowd to assemble below the window of his bedroom at his chateau and provided a barrel of wine for them to celebrate with him the repudiation of the slur upon his renowned prowess. But ... time went by... The crowd waited and waited... The barrel of wine was broached anyway... Advice was shouted up at the window of a kind that more than justified the fears of the Church about 'exciting the lewdness of the multitude'. He got nought out of ten from the three old wives.

The report does not mention the part played by the Countess. Perhaps she just lay back and thought of France. But the Church had had enough. Rome decreed an end to impotence trials.

*

Boy singers are sopranos before their voices break. Up until the nineteenth century in Italy, before the practice was prohibited, some of the best boy sopranos were castrated so that their voices did not break and they remained sopranos into adulthood. They were the *castrati*. Some of them became more famous singers than the leading women sopranos of the day. Although they had women's voices the castrati were fully male in other respects and so were also eagerly sought after as lovers by certain rich women. This was because, being sterile, they could not make women pregnant, whereas normal men disliked using the rather coarse condoms of the time which were made from sheep's intestines, and, unlike modern ones, reduced sensation.

*

Eunuchs – castrated men – played an important part in the affairs of Eastern rulers up until modern times. Some of them became leading ministers or even generals. But they must have been castrated originally to serve as keepers of the harem until their other abilities were noticed. Sometimes the ruler had such large harems that he could not possibly attend to all the women, some of whom were so bored and frustrated that they used the services of the eunuchs. Although there are records of eunuchs being executed for this, there are other instances where the ruler must have known what was going on but turned a blind eye. After all, he was required to bring about male heirs to his throne which may have made demands enough on his virility.

*

Saint Paul, the arch puritan, was so disapproving of sex that he only reluctantly allowed it to be necessary for procreation but then only within marriage. Those doing it outside marriage he consigned to the flames of hell. It is hard to believe that he was unacquainted with the books of the Old Testament. So what did he – or for that matter, people like him such as our present-day Bible thumpers – make of the 'Song of Solomon', especially chapter seven?:

> ... the joints of thy thighs are like jewels ... thy navel is like a round goblet ... thy two breasts are like two young roes ... thine eyes are like the fishpools in Heshbon ... how fair and how pleasant art thou, oh love, for delights...

Gold

It might surprise some people to learn that gold is the commonest of the metals and occurs almost everywhere – there will be tiny amounts in the soil of your garden. But precisely because it is so widely distributed, it is only in few places that it is economic to mine. A man in Northern Ireland heard that some streams flowing into Lough Neagh had gold in their beds. He decided to try panning for it, which entailed shaking the river-bed material through a sieve. And indeed after about a week he had got out about an ounce of gold. Impressive? Well, it had taken about forty hours' panning. He would have earned at least as much labouring on a building site, working half as hard. When Princess Diana married Charles, Prince of Wales, certain Welsh rivers were panned for gold and they did indeed get enough Welsh gold to make Diana a tiara. It was the same story as in Northern Ireland. The panners would have earned more navvying. But that did not put off others who heard about it and eagerly engaged in the back-breaking toil. Nor were the men who took part in the nineteenth-century gold rush to the Klondyke put off by the fact that only a few of them would make fortunes. The madams running brothels and the bar owners made more money than most of the miners, but the rush continued, such is the mesmerising power of gold.

I was mesmerised by it myself for a while when I worked in a City office near the UK's main gold bullion dealers, Brinks Matt, at the end of Leather Lane. Before I describe my own experience of being mesmerised, let me say how

I would sometimes have to wait on the pavement while an armoured truck came out. It could have been carrying not only bullion for banks but gold for workshops making jewellery, cases for watches, Lord Mayors' chains of office, gold leaf for the titles on book covers and much else. There was a small door on the side serving a tiny compartment in which a guard with the keys to the vehicle sat with a loaded gun and which did not open from the outside. I was told that only once did an armed gang ambush it and smash open the little compartment, but the guard opened fire first, killing one of them and wounding another, while the other two fled. The police tried to charge the guard with murder and must have been surprised to learn that the guard was authorised to do what he did.

Brinks Matt began selling gold kruggerrands to the public, each an ounce of pure gold. I bought two of them at about two hundred pounds each, attracted by the terms. These were that Brinks Matt would buy the coins back at the value for gold cited on the Stock Exchange for the day. I gather they made their profit from people taking them back after falls in the Stock Exchange price for gold. For the only time in my life I looked at the City share pages of the paper every day. At home I used to take them out to admire them. Then one day I suddenly asked myself why am I behaving like a gloating miser in one of Dickens' novels? It would never have occurred to me to gloat over a wad of banknotes or a cluster of precious stones! Nor to anyone else. But gold is somehow different in the mesmerising effect it has on everybody.

Nothing could illustrate this more aptly than what happened when the Royal Mint issued a limited number of sovereigns, with the coin equivalent of a watermark to stop them being forged. But they were forged, in places like Abu Dhabi, though – of course – without the 'watermark'. And they found buyers, attracted by stories of them being acquired dubiously, perhaps even stolen, to account for them being offered at much less than the Mint prices. The buyers thought they were being careful by having the coins tested beforehand for purity, and were delighted when they were shown to be genuine twenty-two-carat gold – forgetting about the 'watermark', and so getting per coin fifty pounds' worth of gold for which they had paid over a hundred pounds. I understand that this scam is still going on. Guess who are some of the people who are taken in by it? Yes. Coin dealers!

Perhaps the mesmerising power of gold owes something to two facts about it. One is that it does not occur as an ore that has to be smelted but is found already gleaming brightly. The other is related to the fact that it does not tarnish like silver. Servants in stately homes spent many hours polishing the silver dining cutlery, but gold keeps its alluring shine even after centuries buried in a cesspit. The word 'gold' itself is used to signify quality or achievement. A golden wedding. A golden opportunity. And, of course, the little girl who promises, but does not always manage, to be as good as gold.

Irishness

I had to have a novel published at my own expense by what is called the vanity press. The first vanity press publisher I approached quoted me £8,000 for 500 hardback copies, which was out of the question, but I eventually found an outfit which did me 300 paperback copies for £2,000 in 1995.

I had previously been published in the normal way. My first novel, *The Last Romantic Out of Belfast*, a rough draft of which had lain around for years, was published in 1984 by Blackstaff Press. It had enthusiastic reviews in both London and Dublin and was a runner-up for the David Higham Prize for Fiction. Professor Valentine Cunningham, the well-known media literary pundit, has used it in lectures at Corpus Christi College, Oxford. The David Higham agency took me on and I had no difficulty in getting a collection of short stories titled *The Streets of Laredo* brought out in 1986 by Jonathan Cape, considered to be London's most prestigious publisher.

So why, over a period of years, could I not find a publisher for my next novel, *Lilliburlero*, and had to publish it at my own expense in 1995? It could not be the quality. Vanity press books are rarely reviewed but I did get reviews in the papers I sent it to, including the *Observer*. I sold about 200 copies. Patricia Craig, the critic and writer whose books are published by Oxford University Press, wrote: '. . . an extraordinary book . . . funny, clever, authentic . . . many passages and incidents to savour . . . a wonderfully phantasmagoric finale . . . I will read this book again and again.' Here are some brief extracts:

Two parents, four grandparents ... thirty two great great great grandparents ... one hundred and twenty eight great great great great great great grandparents ... and all their heirs, scions, litters, spawns, lineage ... families patriarchal, families matrilineal, close families, falling out families, offshoots, branches, throwbacks. All these are my begetting.

Popery-hating shipwrights. Shipwright-denouncing true blue boilermakers. Skivvy-groping sons of the manse. Old school brotherhood-of-man-believing Keir Hardy revering toolmaker trade unionists ... Tropical fish fancying Orange Lodge Masters. Dickens loving gas meter readers. Bible thumping wife beaters. One-armed parley-voo Somme survivors. Last chance till-tempted barmen. Church music loving God-doubting bespoke shoemakers...

'And all that was ours on it coloured red,' he mused nostalgically, recalling the Belfast schoolrooms of his boyhood and the British Empire in red on the oilskin maps of the world, London at its heart and money at the heart of London ... *Pitman's Commercial English* ... he had kept his copy for old time's sake. For clerks at the height of Empire ... still used in the twilight of Empire. Clerks in the mill offices of Belfast learnt punctuation, the use of the semi-colon, the letter of enquiry, the reply to complaint, the salutation, the complimentary close...

... while out on the dance floor brylcreemed dog fancier Freezy Fitzsimmons, pencil moustached, patent shoed, many partnered bachelor, suavely executed a Buenos Aires brothel dance based upon the bullfight, to the disapproval of unpartnered callow youth...

Miss Pym's class. Miss Pym, sprung from a noble sire,

seed of Zeus, earth shaker. Fitzsimmons minor, fleet of foot, Sammy Jackson of the loud war cry, Edna of the braided Tresses, Stanley, pale of face, stricken by Eros, Sid Gorman, favourite of Poseidon, destroyer of ships, Cissie Coulter, steadfast in virginity, Nina, fair tressed nymph, Lorna, comliest of maidens, Bertie Marlow of the evil counsel ... come here till I tell you about Bertie Marlow...

...why, I asked her, if she could be British Jewish, could I not be British Irish? Because, she said, the Irish people don't want to be British. Which Irish people, I said. Are the Irish Protestants not a people too? And we argued for hours about what is a people, what is a nation, what is a culture.

The reviews give a clue as to why it was shunned by publishers:

'...a sense of a distinct Irish Protestant culture emerges...' *Observer*

'...a tour de force ... to contain and express the Protestant imagination...' *Fortnight* magazine

Conor Cruise O'Brien has written about '...the cultural arrogance of Catholic Ireland ... [how it] confers the status of honorary Catholic Ireland on those from the protestant culture who pass the test of Irishness by renouncing Britishness.' My first novel *The Last Romantic Out of Belfast* and my short stories were – unintentionally – ambiguous on that point and you could read what you liked into them, though I was taken aback when a Belfast Catholic admirer of the novel wrote to say that he had taken copies to two prisons – by implication for Republican prisoners (I never learnt what they made of it). But *Lilliburlero* is very different, as the above quotes from reviews indicate. In England, the literary world, like the English left, has long had a romantic attachment to Irish nationalism. I recall years ago, when I first came to London, meeting socialists who would not hear a word against the awful bigot de Valéra who kept Eire neutral in the Second World War, censored news about the Germans including the discovery of Auschwitz and sent condolences to the German Embassy on the death of Hitler. Hence there is unspoken but nevertheless great pressure on writers and poets from the Protestant culture to be sympathetic to Irish nationalism. The Opsahl Commission on the Northern Ireland problem some years ago was told by a Jackie Redpath that 'Protestant poets and writers rubbish their culture and almost refuse to admit they belong to it... The well-known poet James Simmons from a Protestant background wrote to me admiring *The Last Romantic* but was later 'saddened' by *Lilliburlero*. At about the same time he said in an interview that he was writing a memoir about his upbringing and would call it 'A Childhood in the Colony'. That word 'colony' would certainly confirm his status as honorary Catholic. The *Fortnight* review of *Lilliburlero* quoted above was, I discovered, by the poet Damian Smyth using a pseudonym, presumably not wishing to use his real name praising a book which, as he puts it, is 'a powerful cocktail of British and Protestant culture...'

It was not always like this. Writers from the Irish Protestant culture at one time had no more difficulty with being also British than the Welsh or the Scots. But this changed gradually with the rise of Catholic nationalism and finally ended in the 1930s when de Valéra, at the same time as he laid claim to Northern Ireland, proclaimed his ambition to make Ireland 'the most Catholic country in the world'. So what did he have in mind for the million northern Protestants in a united Ireland? The answer would appear to be assimilation, or, as it was put proudly by a Catholic Irish woman acquaintance of my (English) wife some years ago: 'We'd marry into them and get the children' (children of mixed marriages are obliged by the Irish Catholic Church to be brought up Catholics or the Catholic partner will be denied the sacrament). This worked in the Republic, where, at independence, Protestants were at least 10 per cent (some put it as high as 20 per cent) of the population and are now virtually extinct. It is unlikely this would work in Northern Ireland since the million Protestants are not a scattered community as were the southern Protestants, who had restricted opportunities for finding partners within it, but obviously de Valéra believed otherwise, as most of Catholic Ireland still does.

But if nationalists did not win territorially there is one sense in which they did win – the welding together of the words 'Irish' and 'Catholic' in the minds of people nearly everywhere outside Ireland.

Some years ago, at a Labour Party social event (my wife was a party member), a man, learning I was from Northern Ireland, assumed I would be pleased to be told that the British should get out of Northern Ireland, and when I told him I was happy to be British he wondered indignantly how a Paisleyite like me could support the Labour Party. In fact, there are tens of thousands of Northern Irish Protestants who would vote Labour if they were not denied the opportunity by the Labour Party refusing to organise in Northern Ireland for fear of offending the Catholic Irish vote in England.

Last year I thought I would try to get my first novel *The Last Romantic Out of Belfast* republished, to help get *Lilliburlero* a proper publisher. I had noticed that books less acclaimed had been republished after shorter periods. When I approached Lilliput Press of Dublin, its publisher, Antony Farrell, wrote saying, 'Indeed I know of your distinguished novel and would be pleased to consider it for republication...' But then he went cold on it, saying, 'reissues are difficult...' It was subsequently turned down by all the publishers I tried. Anne Tannahill, the manager of its original publisher, Blackstaff Press, wrote that, while it is a book she has always greatly admired, sales would not meet production costs. So, twenty years after its publication, the reissue of a book about which reviewers used words like 'marvellous' and phrases like 'verging on greatness' would not sell enough to cover production costs. *Sic transit gloria mundi*! But *Lilliburlero* even more deserved its – as the American artist Andy Warhol put it – ten minutes of fame, but it fell foul of political correctness. This probably put me so beyond the pale that my previous books cannot be reissued except at my own expense and what else I have written will obviously never be published.

He dreams. He is wandering the streets of a semi-strange city that might be London. He comes to a station that might be a tube station. There is moss on the steps leading up to it and water trickles down over the dark stone with hollows worn by feet...

...the Secular Society preacher with the portable pulpit from Speaker's Corner in Hyde Park pushes anti-God tracts into hands outstretched from the train windows ... another tract describes the case of a citizen of protestant Belfast who, though an unbeliever from the age of four, nevertheless grew up with an addiction to the King James bible and tuneful hymns for which cures have proved only temporary and relapses frequent especially with drink taken...

...I land. Island. Ireland. Godland. Prodland. Prayland. Sayland. Nayland. Norland. Nor Ireland. Not Ireland.

Scot Ireland. Prot Ireland. My not Ireland yet Ireland bit Ireland Brit Ireland. I unbelieving bit Brit Ireland leaving elsewhere dwelling far wandering Ireland rememberer.

... the things from his locker went into a cardboard box ... a book of Gospel Hymns by Ira D Sankey ... fifty favourite pub songs with piano accompaniment ... two old postcards: one of the R.M.S. *Titanic*, the other of the biggest linen mill in the world ... a half full bottle of gin ...

Drink

Alcohol is produced by yeast fermenting sugar or starch and occurs naturally. Bees have been observed making an unsteady line back to the hive, after coming away from the blooms of certain flowers. Bears have been seen definitely the worse for wear after a clearly enjoyable session supping from the hollows in trees with syrupy sap.

It is not known when humans learnt about this natural process and how to bring it about in larger quantities, but it was certainly one of the earliest discoveries, long before the wheel. Beer may have arrived before wine – it was included in the rations served to the men building the earliest pyramids over four thousand years ago. Wine is referred to in the Old Testament, not always approvingly. But spirits are a comparatively recent arrival, dating only from a few hundred years ago. Despite their recent arrival, however, little is known about exactly when or how they first came to be produced. Until the fourteenth century only beer and wine were drunk.

Unlike fermentation, which occurs in nature, spirits are a man-made invention, produced by boiling off the vapour from a fermented solution and condensing it by cooling in a process called distillation. Just when and how this process was discovered is unclear. It is thought to have been known to the makers of perfumes and medicines a long time before it became a drink. But when or why it occurred to people to try drinking it remains a mystery. It cannot be because of its taste. It is, in fact, tasteless, and raw spirit in the mouth has a stinging bite which most people would find unpleasant undiluted, unlike beer or wine. The discovery of its more rapid effect than beer or wine can have come about only by some people persisting in imbibing it, despite its unappealing taste. But when word of this effect got about it did catch on rapidly.

But whereas fermentation produces only one form of alcohol – ethyl alcohol – distilling also results in other alcohols such as butyl and propyl, which are actually poisonous, and need to be carefully removed. If this is not done successfully, then there can occur events such as happened recently in India where a dozen men died and many more went blind from drinking a batch of incompetently produced spirit. These poisonous alcohols can be removed during distillation because of their different boiling points. It is easy to see how this might be done in modern distilleries by men in white coats, yet it must also have been done successfully not only by the early makers of spirits but by, for example, the present-day illegal makers of poteen in Ireland, however crude their equipment appears to be, since there have been no reports of horrific poisonings as in India.

Gin was the most popular spirit in early eighteenth-century England, so much so that one of the artist Hogarth's most celebrated pictures is titled *Gin Lane*. It depicts a scene of taverns and street drunkenness, including, strikingly, a woman grinning tipsily as she holds a glass at the top of a flight of steps with her suckling baby falling unheeded from her breast. The taverns are shown attracting customers with the promise of 'Drunk for a penny, dead drunk for tuppence'.

The government of the day decided to take action. It introduced a swingeing tax on spirits but not on beer. Although it is one thing to pass a law, another to enforce it, enforced it certainly was by a newly created office of government called 'Customs and Excise'. The cry 'The excise men are upon us' was heard throughout the land, and many the landlord of an inn was roused from his bed after midnight to find himself looking down the barrel of a gun. Drunkenness declined sharply. The striking thing about this episode in English history is that this decisive action was taken by – in the words used at the time – 'a government of placemen and nobodies', which would seem to show that, at times of national crisis, the most unlikely people can sometimes exercise effective leadership.

The next big change in the regulation of the sale of alcohol came many years later and was, of course, the laws governing drinking establishments. The state of affairs in which any house or room could be used for the sale of alcoholic drinks was ended. Such premises now needed a licence, the issue of which could be objected to by local residents. It is not clear if this licensing was connected to taverns changing their name to 'public houses'. Was it to mark the difference between drinking in houses for purely social purposes and houses in which it was offered for sale? Up until recent times it was not uncommon to see above a public house the words 'licensed for the public consumption of beer and spirits'.

We are now becoming so accustomed to licensed drinking establishments being allowed to choose their own times of doing business that it is being forgotten how recent this is and how strictly regulated these times once were. Eleven a.m. to 10 p.m. weekdays, and on Sundays 12 p.m. to 2 p.m. and 7 p.m. to 10 p.m. with twenty minutes allowed for 'drinking-up time'. These times were strictly enforced. The barman's cry 'Time please' was heard simultaneously in every public house in the land. I recall once being with a group where we were encouraged to drink up by a barman at our table pointedly emptying our ashtray so as to create a cloud of cigarette ash.

But for the most famous or most infamous episode in

the history of drinking we go America – Prohibition. American culture has always had a puritanical streak, and just after the First World War the puritans – especially church-going Protestants – at last got their way and public drinking was made illegal.

But, unlike licensing laws, Prohibition was impossible to enforce. It is hard now to understand why anyone thought it could be. All over America no one had any difficulty in getting a drink. It is reckoned that during Prohibition there were more illegal bars or 'speakeasies' (where you knocked three times and asked *quietly* for Joe) than there had been legal ones before Prohibition. Ships hove to just outside national waters after dark and fast launches carried their cargoes of wines and spirits ashore to waiting trucks. On the Canadian frontier, truck drivers tucked dollars into the pockets of customs officials to turn a blind eye to their loads. The dealers were called bootleggers. In one of Scott Fitzgerald's famous novels, *The Great Gatsby*, a lavish party is thrown by the big-time bootlegger Gatsby at his mansion, attended by everybody who was anybody, including – of course – the local police chief.

Prohibition also virtually created the mafia, or at least the American version of it. It may come as a surprise to many that the mafia originated in Sicily as an admirable organisation, set up to defend the interests of the peasants against oppressive landowners. It may come as an even greater surprise to know that a shade of its noble origins still flickered in the American mafia in the 1930s, the time of the Great Depression (Buddy, can you spare a dime?). A limousine would draw up at a church hall in the Italian quarter of New York and out of it would step a mafia big-time mobster in a camel-hair coat accompanied by his moll in furs and a wad of banknotes in his pocket with which he would distribute handouts to the unemployed Italian American men in the hall. This partly explains why the authorities' difficulty in prosecuting the mobsters (Al Capone was convicted for non-payment of income tax) was not entirely due to intimidation.

Another surprise might be why whiskey is a brown colour and not clear like gin or vodka. In fact, when distilled it is indeed clear, but, unlike gin or vodka, even the best freshly distilled whiskey has unpleasant side flavours which can only be got rid of by leaving it to 'mature' for long periods of up to ten years. This maturing was originally done in old sherry casks imported from Spain. These were so saturated with dried-out sherry that they imparted a brown colour to the whiskey. When whiskey production increased so much that the distilleries could not get enough sherry casks they started maturing it in stainless-steel tanks instead, in which it of course remained clear. But by then people the world over had got so used to the brown colour that the distilleries could not wean them off it, despite publicised tastings. So the distillers still have to add a brown tasteless dye to the natural clear colour of the world's most famous spirit or people will not buy it. 'If it ain't brown, it ain't whiskey.'

Surely the wine world is free of such absurdities? Or is it? What about the fuss made of regions and vintages? Some years ago a panel of wine experts was tested on their ability to select the best wines from groups of unlabelled but numbered bottles. They started off being asked to pick out a bottle priced £10.99 among others priced £3.99, which they did easily. But then so would we. However, when it was the £20.99 among a lot at £10.99 and so on up the price range they began to get it wrong and ended up with right decisions that could have been the same from guesses. So much for the high-flown jargon of wine buffs. Then there was the millionaire with the bottle of Château Lafitte so rare it cost him £2,000. He opened it and tasted it to a packed audience on a televised performance.

Well, of course, if you taste wine from a £2,000 bottle, you have to do more than say it is very nice or even smack your lips. So he did a great deal more. The pleasure convulsed him. He writhed in ecstasy. He emitted gasps and cries as if having an overpowering orgasm... The studio audience looked at each other. I don't know what the TV audience made of it.

But let us not be too hard on wine lovers, seeing that the most celebrated of them has written poetry about wine that has given pleasure to us all in the beautiful translation by Edward Fitzgerald of the *The Rubaiyat of Omar Khayyám.* Yet it was not primarily as a poet that Omar was famous in the Persia of his day (1048–1141) but as an astronomer and mathematician. His calendar is almost as accurate as that of today. The Greeks invented geometry but the Arabs and Persians, led by Omar Khayyám, invented algebra (*al-Gebr* – the system of reckoning). What senior schoolboys doing mathematics know as the binomial theorem – the expansion of (a + b) to the power *n* – is also known as Omar Khayyám's theorem. His poetry, on the other hand, was little known in his own time, though it got him into trouble for its subversive enthusiasm for drinking not only as an escape from narrow-minded conventions but as an expression of agnostic doubt about religion, as shown in the following two of its many verses:

The Grape that can with logic absolute
The Two And seventy jarring sects confute
The Subtle alchemist that in a trice
Life's leaden metal into gold transmute.

*

Into this universe and why not knowing
I came like water willy nilly flowing
And out of it as wind along the waste
I know not whither, Willy nilly blowing.

Omar Khayyám had to leave the court, and his life might have been in danger had his friends not persuaded him to make a pilgrimage to Mecca he did not believe in.

It was not only powerful forces in his own age that he upset by challenging their conventional beliefs – the Victorians did not like him much either. But let us give old Omar the last word on the subject of drink:

And when Thee oh death with shining foot shall pass
Among the guests star scattered on the grass,
And in thy joyous errand reach the Spot
Where I made one – turn down an empty glass.

CHEERS!

QWERTY

QWERTY. The first five letters on the keyboard of the typewriter since the typewriter was invented in the latter part of the nineteenth century and the term used for the whole keyboard arrangement. This is used in every country employing the Roman alphabet with only minor differences for other non-letter characters such as accents etc., as in France for example, so that typists going to different countries do not need retraining.

In the 1930s an American university decided to find out if another keyboard arrangement would be more efficient, that is, would enable typists to type faster. It came up with the surprising discovery (I do not know anything about the methodology used except that it was never questioned) that *any* other arrangement would be faster, including a random one!

Could this have been accidental? Out of the countless keyboard arrangements of letters could the least efficient, QWERTY, have just been hit upon by chance? The manufacturers of typewriters were of no help. The first makers of typewriters had kept no records. But someone on the university team had a hunch which proved correct. An examination of still-existing models of early typewriters showed that they were not as robust as they later became and were easily damaged by fast typing. So QWERTY had actually been designed to slow typists down!

This discovery prompted the suggestion that QWERTY should be abandoned. This met with little interest until the Second World War, or rather at the point when America entered it. It was then realised that the enormous expansion of record-keeping would mean that the number of new typists needed would be greater than the number of existing ones and could be trained just as easily on a faster keyboard. But while the proposal was seriously considered, it was not taken up, as there were more pressing decisions to be made.

About twenty years after the war came computers and the beginning of word processing. Typists in the bigger companies no longer typed onto paper but onto screens and sent the result to a printer. But it was the proliferation of personal computers and, eventually, the laptop that really made typewriters as obsolete as steam locomotives on the railways.

People adapt so quickly to change that it is now almost forgotten what life was like before the computer for anybody in the business of writing for or publishing books or newspapers. While most writers like me had our small portable typewriters on which we did a certain amount of two-finger typing for letters and so forth, our stuff for publishers – i.e. our typescripts, which publishers still call manuscripts – had to be well presented and error free and so I, for example, had to send my hand written manuscript to a typing agency. But not today. Writers and journalists can now compose their work on a computer screen at home, unworried about errors or spelling mistakes, which can be easily corrected later in a final draft, before sending to the printer. The need for typing agencies must have nearly disappeared.

This huge proliferation of keyboards was foreseen from the day IBM introduced the first cheap home computer. This brought another call for QWERTY to be replaced by a faster keyboard, this time reinforced by calculations of the millions of hours saved, even in the USA alone. But the demand was again seen off. Both lost opportunities to replace QWERTY are now represented as examples of progress being hindered by vested interests and conservatism. But this, while seemingly plausible, does not really stand up if you think about it. The economic savings would be only be realised after a costly period of transition. The changeover would have to be brought in gradually otherwise big companies and government typing pools would be at a standstill for weeks. Think of the worldwide retraining of QWERTY typists, who, as well as having to learn a new keyboard, would also have to resist an almost automatic urge to hit a wrong key (bear in mind that professional typists are touch-typists and do not look at the keyboard) and would therefore be liable to make more mistakes than new trainees.

So, like it or lump it, we are stuck with nineteenth-century QWERTY for evermore.

Rape

Rape is different to all other crimes. It involves an act which can also be one of pleasure. If someone is apprehended breaking into your house, the culprit cannot claim that you invited him to do it, that you enjoyed it, which is the classic rapist's defence in court. But while that is its most obvious difference to all other offences, there are other differences. There was the recent outrage expressed by women at the home secretary saying that some rapes were less serious than others. Yet he could have said that about any other crime including murder and no one would have disagreed.

Then there is the question: what kind of men commit it?

The idea that rapists are men who cannot get women in the normal way, whether because of physical or some other form of personal unattractiveness, does not stand up to the most cursory consideration of cases either in the news or notoriously known.

Take, for example, the recent sensational case of Dominique Strauss-Kahn, top man at the International Monetary Fund, who stood trial in New York for the attempted rape of a hotel chambermaid who fled from his room in distress claiming he had attacked her. He is French and his arrest caused outrage in France where he was considered to be the favourite to win the next election for the presidency, which of course he can not now put himself up for. All sorts of prominent people in France angrily challenged the validity of the charge for many reasons, including American anti-French prejudice. But in the chorus of outrage in France – mostly from men – over Strauss-Kahn, there emerged a picture of French male attitudes to sex which shocked the rest of the world. Their defence of Strauss-Kahn was that a man in his position did not need to rape a black chambermaid, since all-powerful French politicians had as many mistresses as they wanted. Indeed, so much is it expected of them to have mistresses that if any of them are happily married they have to pretend to have one. There are even agencies in France who will supply beautiful women to be seen in hotels and restaurants in the company of prominent men to counter any suspicions about their normality or their manhood. The hotel maid, it seems, should have been flattered – an attitude in which the rest of the world perceived a more than lingering trace of the old pre-Revolution aristocrat's *droit de seigneur* over female underlings.

But something else became public about Strauss-Kahn more to the point about the question 'Why do men rape?' It was the remarks made about him by some of the many other women he had had sex with. They were persuaded to go public, supposedly to demonstrate further that he was so attractive to women he had no need to rape a menial. But these ex-lovers mentioned that he did like to be 'a bit rough despite their protests'. Only a few commentators picked up the significance of this. Being rough added spice to his pleasure and, had they not just protested but physically resisted him, it would have added even more. In other words, rapists are men for whom the need for violence is a turn-on. Let us look at some men who prove this.

Beria was the second most powerful man in the Soviet Union after Stalin, responsible for the execution of thousands and the filling up of the labour camps – the Gulag, as the whole system was called. At Stalin's overthrow, he was tried and shot almost immediately. At his trial there emerged details of him as a voracious rapist. At night he would cruise the streets of Moscow in his armoured limousine preying upon good-looking women whom his thugs would snatch for him to take away and rape. But why? A man in his position would have had no need to do that to get women. It is well known that there are women – a minority certainly but more than a tiny few – who are turned on by male celebrity of any kind, whether footballers or politicians, to whom they write to offer themselves enclosing photos. The secretaries of famous men have to sort out these letters from their in-trays nearly every day. In Beria's case, there would have been, in addition to these, the offers from the womenfolk of men on trial facing death or the labour camp. He would have been spoilt for choice. But he would not have got the kicks from them he got from rape.

And how about Tolstoy? Do I hear you gasp in disbelief? The great author of *Anna Karenina* and *War And Peace* a rapist? Sorry, but we have his own word for it. When he got married he presented his bride with his diary, saying there should be no secrets between man and wife. What he thought his wife should read was that when he was a youth his mother, the Countess, sent him a serf girl on their great estate for him to use to lose his virginity, saying that a young man should know about such things before he went to the court at St Petersburg. For the rest of his youth his favourite pastime was to go to the serf quarters and take out a serf girl to throw on the grass and rape. But the angry response of his wife – by now a Countess as he had become Count Tolstoy – was even more shocking. She let it be known that Tolstoy knew no other way of making love to her than throwing her onto the bed and raping her – the great author of *Anna Karenina*, the favourite book of many women, because – as I once heard a group of women say, 'it shows that he understands women'.

It was only as recently as the late nineteenth century that the law recognised the right of a wife to say no to a husband. Even an estranged husband could not be charged with rape. It was not even allowed as grounds for divorce for which only proven adultery was allowed.

I will end on a somewhat controversial note about rape. When the Russian army overran eastern Germany in the closing stages of the Second World War many thousands of German women were raped. However, some said that they did not deserve much sympathy because those Russian soldiers came from a country in which nearly 20 million people had been killed by the German army – that is, by the menfolk, the husbands, sons and brothers of those women – so that those Russian soldiers actually showed great forbearance in only raping them.

Fame

Fame comes in many forms. Fame that comes early, fame that comes late, fame that is eagerly sought after, fame that is unwelcome, fame that is merited, fame that is undeserved, fame that is permanent, fame that is fleeting.

It has been said that people are truly famous when their names are known to everybody and not just to those interested in why they are famous. They are what might be called the permanently famous. Thus everybody has heard of people like Shakespeare, Hitler, Napoleon... They might be classified as belonging to the first division of the permanently famous. In the second division of that category are those who, though famous for all time, not quite everybody will immediately remember, such as Marco Polo, Madam Curie, Sylvia Pankhurst... Then there are the fleetingly famous, those who suddenly burst upon the world stage in a blaze of publicity and then quickly fade away again.

There is a story told about James Cagney, the Hollywood film star. He had a friend who got tired of forever hearing Cagney complaining about how awful it was to be so well known he could never go anywhere without attracting unwelcome attention, and how lucky his friend was in being able, for example, to enjoy a meal in a restaurant without being gawped at. His friend called one evening and said he had booked a table at a top restaurant for them. Well, Cagney said, you won't like the attention I'll get. His friend produced from a bag an old jacket that was badly scuffed and a pair of ugly wire-framed round glasses, and made Cagney put them on.

When they arrived he also ruffled Cagney's well-groomed hair to make it untidy. Cagney came back in a bad temper. Because he had been stared at? No, because he had *not*.

Cagney was not unusual among the famous in both wanting the attention their celebrity brings them and at the same time wanting to be able to go for a drink and a meal just like the rest of us. They would like to be able to turn their celebrity on and off like something out of a tap. They want it both ways.

Of course, it could be said that there was a time when the famous did indeed have it both ways and could be famous in name but not in person. Take, for example, Charles Dickens. It has today been forgotten just how unique his fame as a writer was. He is the only great writer whose readership extended to the working class, who, in the words of the day, was read from the cottage to the palace. He gave readings to halls packed with thousands – when, for instance, he read about the death of Little Nell everyone cried, he cried, they all had a good cry together. His publisher published his books in weekly newspaper instalments before the books came out. When a ship docked in America, people on the dock would be there to ask about what was happening to his latest misfortune-threatened character. Yet Dickens could walk the streets unrecognised and took train journeys just like anyone else, which would today be inconceivable for anyone of such celebrity.

Things began to change, though gradually, as the demands of industrialisation meant that the working classes had to be literate enough to read instructions about machinery and were hence also able to read mass-circulation newspapers. Then came the invention of the camera and press photographers, the development of the moving image, the birth of the film industry, the appearance of not only actors in movies but of the famous in newsreels, not only in cinemas but, as today, on TVs in every household in the country. If, today, anyone does anything newsworthy, they will answer the doorbell not just to a newspaper reporter but to a TV crew.

Yet something else has also changed: public attitudes to the famous. They are no longer considered to have any right to the privacy that in the past they would have been granted. This is illustrated by a story told of old Vienna. An English visitor was walking in a park with a Viennese friend who pointed out to him a rather smallish ugly-faced man walking alone nearby. That is the great Beethoven, the Viennese friend told him proudly but in a low voice so as not to be overheard by Beethoven. In Washington, the President could once walk from the White House to the Congress building with only a few people accompanying him.

Fame is addictive, and, like all addictions, can be destructive. Dickens did not give those public readings of his stories for the money but for the thrill of seeing in front of him his adoring readers. It left him exhausted. His doctor warned him to stop it, but he could not, because he was addicted. It probably killed him at the early age of fifty-eight.

But we nowadays have a new category among the famous brought about by the change in pop music. At one time pop music appealed to all ages. Old bricklayers on building sites would be heard whistling the latest popular tune, from Sinatra and Elvis to the Beatles. But today when singing has been superseded by shouting, which is itself nearly drowned by the deafening rhythm, it is only the young who listen to it and we have pop stars and bands whose concerts need the police to control the crush of fans but whose names are unknown to anyone over the age of about twenty-five.

The pursuit of fame has something in it akin to why

religion has such appeal: the human craving for the promise of something that will persist beyond the end of life, of life being something more than – as Omar Khaayám put it – that which, 'like snow upon the desert's dusty face, lighting a little hour or two, is gone.'

Evil

The Holocaust is without doubt the worst atrocity that has ever been perpetrated in the history of humanity. Yet it is worth looking into just why it stands out as unique. Man's inhumanity to man is all too common throughout history. In the Roman Empire, cruelty in the arena was laid on for public entertainment and public crucifixion was a not uncommon method of executing criminals. In the UK, up till comparatively recent times, people – including children – could be hanged for petty theft before thousands of spectators. Even on the larger scale there were massacres involving huge numbers such as when the Romans suppressed a Jewish revolt and put to the sword all the people of Jerusalem, or when the Romans themselves were overrun by the armies of Attila the Hun and Rome was sacked. Then in our own times the birth of the countries Pakistan and India was attended by Hindus and Muslims slaughtering hundreds of thousands of each other. Indeed, the Jews themselves had long known persecution involving massacres, including one in the city of York in the fourteenth century, but especially in the pogroms that not infrequently happened in Russia.

So what was so different about the Holocaust, apart from the scale? Even on the point of scale it has to be remembered that the population of the world was much smaller in past times; hence the figures involved in past massacres would have to be multiplied when comparing them proportionately to those of the Holocaust. Then there is the question of why it happened and where. If anyone at the beginning of the twentieth century had been told that a great catastrophe would befall the Jewish people and asked to predict where it would take place, everybody, not least the Jews themselves, would have said Russia because of the notorious pogroms. No one, least of all the Jews, would have named Germany and the Germans. Germany, the country that had produced Beethoven and Bach, the motherland of classical music, that had produced Goethe, considered by many as the equal of Shakespeare, that had produced Karl Marx, the father of idealistic socialism? (From each according to his ability, to each according to his need.) Impossible surely.

So why did it happen in what, at the beginning of the twentieth century, was perhaps the most civilised country in the world, a country, which, unlike the UK or the US, did not have a history stained by institutionalised slavery, a country whose monarchy was closely related to ours and visited by more British people than any other? On top of all that was the fact that intermarriage between Jews and non-Jews was higher than in any other country, so high in fact that when Hitler introduced the Nazi anti-Jewish laws they applied only to those 'with more than one grandparent a Jew'; so many Germans would otherwise have been affected, including, it is said, leading Nazis such as Hermann Goering.

Yet even at the beginning of the century clouds were gathering. Arguments still go on as to what started the Anglo-German naval race to build the biggest battleships. But the utterly unexpected happened and we had the 1914–18 war, and Germany's catastrophic defeat. But what followed the defeat was even worse for the Germans than the defeat itself. Fighting, of course, stopped at the Armistice, but because technically the war was not over, the British navy still maintained the blockade of the North Sea ports until the Versailles peace treaty, causing food shortages and even hunger. Then the peace treaty imposed terribly harsh terms, forcing huge reparation payments on Germany for twenty years. It is said that these were at the insistence of the French rather than the rest of the Allies, who were forced to give way rather than 'insult the honour of France'. As well as all that there was the attempt by the communists to stage the easily suppressed workers' revolution in Berlin in 1918. It would seem that the leading communists of the day, especially the exiles in London, had been taken by surprise when the long-awaited revolution of the working class happened in Russia in 1917 and not in Germany as long expected.

A sullen, embittered German population throughout the 1920s nursed grievances for which they wanted somebody to blame. The aborted revolution in 1918 had sent a seismic shock wave through the German middle class which felt that Germany had been 'stabbed in the back'. It is claimed that the fact that many of the leaders of the revolution, such as Rosa Luxemburg, were Jewish and inspired by the Jew Karl Marx may have caused them to turn on the Jews.

However, it was not only the right wing that responded to Hitler's anti-Semitic ranting; so did the working class and indeed much of left-wing Germany. Hitler was so determined to get the backing of the socialists that the very name 'Nazi' for his party is an abbreviation for National *Socialist*.

Whatever the roots and origins of Nazi anti-Semitism, it proved popular. The Nazis had no need to seize power when they did so in 1933. In the previous general election they had won over one-third of the votes and their popularity was increasing so that they would almost certainly have won a majority in another election.

In power they brought in the infamous racial purity laws. Here we have the crucial difference between the Holocaust and previous pogroms and massacres. The Holocaust was not carried out by mobs, inflamed by ranting demagogues, as in the pogroms, but ordered coldly by a government. 'The Final Solution to the Jewish Question' was implemented under Adolf Eichmann. When the Israeli agents tracked him down in Argentina after the war to kidnap him and put him on trial in Israel and hang him, people were surprised to see and hear not a shaven-headed SS thug but a mild-mannered bespectacled senior civil servant who had gone about his task by setting up a huge civil service department to oversee the building of the camps. Filling them involved the studying of railway timetables, the calculations of throughput, and, above all, the sending of civil servants everywhere to examine birth and marriage civil records, looking for *more than one grandparent a Jew*. In offices all over Europe there would have been street maps showing how the work was progressing. The maps would have looked not much different to maps in this country showing the progress of a slum-clearance programme.

In the department's correspondence files are preserved official letters concerning individual cases. One such involved a man visited by officials who left after politely agreeing that the letters he produced showed that his case was still undecided, as it still was when the war ended. The language in these letters is so little different to what would have been used in matters about taxation or building regulations that it is not easy to realise that, since they are concerned with whether he had *more than one grandparent a Jew*, they are in fact about whether he should live or die.

Then there was the odd case when a whole street of non-Jewish Germans was descended upon by officials. This occurred after a carriage of an army hospital train from the Russian front somehow got shunted off the train onto sidings at the back of this street and the death of many of the severely wounded occupants owing to thirst and inattention over the hours before the mistaken shunting was discovered. Had the people in the houses not heard the cries, the official enquiry wanted to know? Oh yes they had heard them, but the enquiry concluded that their explanation of why they had done nothing was not unreasonable. The people had assumed that the shouting was from Jews being transported. So much for the claim that the German people did not know what was happening to the Jews.

There appeared in the dock at the Nuremberg trials an SS man who had received a special commendation from Heinrich Himmler, Hitler's number two and head of the SS. He had made a big saving. The gas used in the gas chambers was in short supply and he had discovered that children needed only half as much as adults so should be gassed in separate batches. The man was youngish, pleasant-looking and soft-spoken. His wife wept when he was sentenced to death, her tears as sincere as those of any other woman about to lose a loved one. His defence was that he was simply doing his job. I suspect that, if he had been ordered to run an orphanage in the ordinary way, his treatment of the children would probably have been exemplary. Perhaps he lived in one of the houses we saw recently on TV. Very charming single-storey houses just outside the site of what had been a death camp. Houses for those of the SS who had families. For family men. Men who could spend a shift exterminating children and then come home to play with their own children.

Then there were the women such as were observed in a scene in wartime Paris marshalling a group of children on a railway station platform. To take them on an outing perhaps? Well, kind of. The children were from orphanages. Meticulous searches of their records had shown them to have *more than one grandparent a Jew* and the seemingly attentive, caring women worked for the SS and were taking them off to be put to death.

It would, of course, be a wild exaggeration to claim that all Germans were involved in the Holocaust. It would not, however, be a wild exaggeration to claim that all Germans knew somebody who was involved, even if only in a clerical capacity, and did not think the less of them for it. There was the huge number of office staff employed by the SS, for example. The families and friends and neighbours must have known what the work of those clerks and typists was about, with their correspondence folders and filing cabinets.

When I was thirteen years old there was a German prisoner-of-war camp near my home town of Lisburn in Northern Ireland. We heard accounts of how well behaved they were, of the carols they sang at Christmas, the toys they made for the guards' children. In the last days of the war a column of them was often allowed out of the camp on a walk in their distinctive uniforms near where I lived, and several times when they passed me I was given a friendly wave, which I returned. Then the local cinema showed the first newsreels of the liberated death camps: the corpses stacked like wood in a timber yard outside the terrible gas chambers, the still-living human skeletons feebly trying to pick vermin from their striped shirt-like garments. I tried to associate those awful newsreels with the decent-looking German POWs who waved to me, but could not. I thereafter avoided passing them on their walks so as to avoid getting a wave. I did not know then that the German-language teacher at my school had had much more contact with them. It was many years later when, as a successful playwright, he wrote about it in a memoir. When those POWs no longer had to stay in a column, one of them passed his gate and he asked him in. The POW visited quite a few times and was much liked by his children. When the newsreels about the death camps showed, he thought he should let the German know he did not hold all Germans accountable for the crimes of Hitler's Nazis.

But he hardly got further than mentioning Hitler's name, seemingly sympathetically, when the POW's face lit up and he spoke eagerly about his beloved Führer. My teacher was shocked and dismayed that they had both got it so wrong about each other. I should add that the POW was from the ordinary German army, the Wehrmacht, not the SS.

That German POW would not have lost his admiration of Hitler when he went back to Germany. A survey of older Germans done many years later was disturbing in its finding of how many of them still thought well of Hitler. There was a TV film about it. One old woman looked very like my mother. When she was shown a picture of Hitler, she said almost lovingly, 'Ach ja, der Führer.' Hitler's terrible achievement was to contaminate a whole population with evil. Nothing could more epitomise that than my final example found in the effects of an old woman when she died. Her son had been killed on the eastern front and she had kept his last letter. In it he described leading the search of a house which the men under him had reported as having been completed. But he was not satisfied and went back into it. His hunch had proved correct. He found a little boy who had been hidden in a broom cupboard. A little *Jewish* boy. It is hard to believe that he saw nothing wrong in writing such a letter to his dear mother, even harder to believe that his dear mother saw nothing wrong in proudly keeping it in loving remembrance of her dear son.

I will end with what I heard a man say when I was in an immigrant hostel in Australia to which I had emigrated under the 'ten pounds scheme'. He was the sole survivor of not only his own family but of a large extended family all of whom had been exterminated in the Holocaust. He was asked what he thought of the many thousands of German civilians who had been killed in the British bombing raids. He answered very simply – 'they didn't kill enough of them.'

The Might-Have-Beens

My working-class father and a lot of people like him believed that nobody ever got a good job through ability alone but through influence, friends at court, or – if the word had been in their vocabulary – nepotism. It's not what you know but who you know, they said.

But they were right only up to a point. I became a head of department in a leading British company. I became that because I was a good administrator – in that I would get promotion for juniors who had ability even if I did not personally like them. I did that, not, or not primarily, from loyalty to the company, but from self-interest. By doing their job well they made my job easier. Exactly the same reason why Eisenhower in 1944 appointed the British general Montgomery commander of the Allied invasion force even though he personally disliked him and the US government wanted him to choose an American.

No big organisation of any kind would survive if it did not promote people of ability. And the fact that people are also promoted for the reasons cited by my father makes that all the more necessary. But then the question arises: promoted to what level? The answer would appear to be: to the *middle*. Nearly everyone of ability gets stuck in the middle and that applies in every field: industry, the armed forces, the Church, the Chinese Communist Party, the theatre, the arts. People of ability will get pushed and promoted to the middle. But that is where the pushing forward stops. Nobody gets pushed from the middle to the top. The problem for people of ability is not getting from the bottom to the top but getting from the middle to the top. Were there any other officers who would have been as good or better than Montgomery if they had not got stuck in the middle? Of course there were. Getting above the middle depends on other factors than ability, the chief one probably being *luck*. If a brilliant young officer was recommended to Napoleon for promotion he would ask, 'But what of his luck. Is his luck good?' One of his junior generals had had a swift rise to that rank because of his brilliance but then upset Napoleon by failing to win a battle. When it was pointed out to Napoleon that this would have happened to any general, as it was due to utterly unforeseeable circumstances, Napoleon replied that it had not happened to any general but to *him*: his luck was not good. He remained stuck in the middle.

And what of Napoleon himself, how did he become … Napoleon? It happened during the Reign of Terror in the French Revolution. Some of the leading revolutionaries accidentally found their names on Robespierre's list of people to be guillotined and organised a coup that saw Robespierre himself guillotined instead. But mobs of the poor poured onto the streets of Paris to exact revenge because Robespierre had given them bread. The coup leaders were desperate until one of them remembered a young captain of artillery called Napoleon Bonaparte who had distinguished himself against the British at the siege of Toulon and who was in Paris. They offered him the command of all the Revolutionary armies in the Paris region with the rank of general. From captain to general at the age of twenty-six and he asked for an hour to think it over! Have you artillery, he asked them, and where was it? He and what soldiers he could muster raced to get it. The mobs had the same idea but the young Napoleon got there first – just – and cleared the streets of Paris in the episode known as 'The Whiff of Grapeshot', after which he went on to become one of the most famous men in history. No wonder he thought luck so important and insisted on his officers' luck being good.

We have the word of William the Conqueror himself that the Battle of Hastings was – as Wellington later said about Waterloo – a damned close-run thing. But were there not others besides William and Wellington who should have got some credit for winning? As is the way with great stories, history has ruthlessly edited out anything or anybody not essential to their resonance. The vital manoeuvre that won the Battle of Trafalgar was mostly conducted by Admiral Collingwood yet it is Nelson who is up there alone on London's most famous landmark. The blind eye, the empty sleeve, the affair with Lady Hamilton, dying nobly on the deck of the *Victory* – Hollywood couldn't have scripted it better!

The tragedy of the *Titanic* made it the most famous ship ever, but it also illustrates how legends are made by editing out whatever gets in the way of a great story. An eyewitness account published by a survivor and still in print refers to its launch as a big event celebrating the building of the greatest ship the world had ever seen. Not true. The *Titanic* had a sister ship, the *Olympic*, which had gone into service a year previously without any more razzmatazz than the usual launching ceremony for any ship. The photos in the advertising material about the *Titanic* featuring the luxurious public rooms, the magnificent staircase and so on were taken aboard the identical *Olympic*. Both ships were built in Belfast where as many men must have worked on the *Olympic*. Belfast went into mourning for the *Titanic* in 1912 after the disaster. Half the parlour walls in the city since then have had a picture of the *Titanic* on the wall and the *Olympic* was forgotten, even though it continued in service till 1935.

When Charles Darwin was delaying publication of his

work on evolution because he feared it would upset his much-loved religious wife, he received a manuscript from another naturalist, Alfred Russell Wallace, asking him to help get it published. Darwin realised that Wallace had got there first. To Darwin's credit, when *On the Origin of Species* came out, Darwin shared the authorship with Wallace. But Darwin had a name already made well known by his philosopher grandfather, Erasmus, so that, while everybody has heard of Darwin's theory, how many know it as also Wallace's?

And what about the great transformation of human affairs brought about by the invention of the printing press. Look it up and only Gutenberg is named, even though there were earlier printers who experimented with trays of forged-steel letters but whose names have been forgotten. And that other great transformation of human affairs – the railways. People had lived and died within ten miles of their village until the railway arrived and they could go to once distant places in a matter of hours to find work when before it would have taken days. Everybody has heard of Stevenson's *Rocket* and Brunel's bridges and tunnels but before them there had been a steam road coach in London that ran successfully between the City and Marble Arch, the boiler heated by smokeless charcoal replenished at stops. There were plans to open a service between towns on main roads now greatly improved by a Scotsman named John McAdam with his newly invented resurfacing material of tar and gravel. But the stagecoach interests used their influence to kill the steam coach off with a law requiring a man to walk in front of it with a red flag, though in fact they should have seen the steam road coach as an ally. Had the stagecoach people been wiser, steam-powered road travel might have given the railways serious competition instead of stagecoaches themselves being killed off by the railways, after which the roads reverted to their previous primitive condition for another fifty years till the arrival of the motor vehicle. The name Macadam is now preserved as the name of a road-making material and the man himself is forgotten as are the name's of the engineers who built the steam coach.

When what was to become the Americas Cup Atlantic Yacht Race was first run round the Isle of Wight, Queen Victoria was ensconced on the cliffs to watch the yachts going past. She heard the boom of cannon and the cheering of the crowds greet the winner. When she was told who it was, she asked, 'And who, pray, is second?' and was told, 'Er, Ma'am, there is no second.'

The poet Gray got it right in his Elegy 'Written in a Country Church-Yard':

Some mute inglorious Milton here may rest,
Some Cromwell guiltless of his country's blood.

But what about all the other cemeteries in which there are not only unknown Miltons but Chaucers, Coleridges, Wordsworths, Tennysons, Popes, Kiplings, even Shakespeares. And what of the artists we could never hear of. I remember the colourful dyehouse in the huge linen spinning mill near Belfast where I first worked. Sometimes a customer would want a further supply of a previous order and they had to match the colour. They used a big rough man in the dyehouse who had what they called 'a great eye'. Is that not what artists have? Was he not what he would never have known himself to be – an artist? And how many others like him? How many other Leonardos, Rembrandts, Constables will we never know about? I once wrote a novel called *The Last Romantic out of Belfast* which was something of a hit. It got enthusiastic reviews in both London and Dublin – the word 'marvellous' was used in several of them. The David Higham literary agency took me on, getting me lined up to sign a contract with the big mass-paperback publisher Corgi. Such publishers only take on a book if they think it will sell at least ten thousand copies, not only in bookshops but also – and perhaps more importantly – in railway stations, airports and even cruise liners. However, the agency had been dealing with the publisher's number two man, its number one being in America. Number one came back and wrote to the agency – I still have a copy of his letter – that, while he greatly admired the book which he thought was beautifully written, its market would be too limited. If that number one man had come back a few days later, the contract would have been signed and he would have had to back its marketing. My luck was not good.

And so I, too, have joined the honourable ranks of the once briefly acclaimed now fading names of the nearlies, the almosts, the might-have-beens.

Down Under

How many Australians know the correct words of 'Waltzing Matilda', their unofficial national anthem? Or rather the correct version of its most important single word – *Matilda.* In the original version composed by the poet Banjo Paterson it is not Matilda but 'my tilda'. He was referring to what out-of-work job seekers were required to do under the Poor Laws brought over from England by the early colonists – keep on the move, which they called 'waltzing'. They 'waltzed' around Australia looking for work with their few belongings carried on a stick over their shoulder in a pack called – for some reason – a 'tilda'. It is 'You'll come a-waltzing my tilda with me'. You can hardly blame the Australians for preferring to waltz with Matilda – we all would. Paterson wrote other poems admired by T.S. Eliot but now forgotten. Yet nothing of Eliot's is as well known as the corrupted words of that great song.

I lived in Australia for about two years in the 1950s, and, as with most immigrants, there were some things I found it hard to adjust to. One was the early onset of darkness in summer. Australia is in the southern hemisphere. It is only in the northern hemisphere that there is the long summer twilight. This does not occur in Australia where at the height of summer it is dark in the evening by half past seven. Since most of the world lives in the northern hemisphere – Japan, China, India, half of Africa, Europe, all North America, part of South America – it is Australia that is an oddity. But another, and probably a more important thing, is its – for want of a better term –

Americanisation. Not only people from this country but all Europeans are used to the big newspapers being *national*, and so find it hard to adjust to them in Australia being *local.* In Melbourne, for example, where I lived, the big daily newspaper, the *Melbourne Herald*, will have in it - like in an American newspaper - mostly local news, with very little about what is going on elsewhere in Australia, unless it is something sensational. This American way of life goes deeper than newspapers. Just as there are many Americans who may have been to Europe but have never been to other well-known parts of America, so there are many Australians who may have been to England but have never been in the Australian Outback. I worked for a time at an open-cast coal mine in Leigh Creek in the Outback halfway to Alice Springs which is in the centre of Australia and so, having also met Aborigines there, had seen more of Australia than most Australians. Despite their fondness for being seen as being like Crocodile Dundee, the bushwacker in the floppy hat, the overwhelming majority are city dwellers to an even greater extent than in any other country. List their cities, starting with the first port of call for ocean liners and then going on round the coast - Perth, Adelaide, Melbourne, Brisbane, Sydney - and you have accounted for 90 per cent of the population. They are, in fact, the most urbanised people in the world.

There is in fact quite a large amount of industry in Australia. After my first job at the open-cast coal mine at Leigh Creek where they were building a huge power station, I then went on to work for Nobels (the Nobel Prizes people) in Melbourne at one of the biggest industrial explosives plants in the world (the Nobel Prizes money comes from the invention of dynamite by a man called Nobel), after which I worked for Monsanto Chemicals - also in Melbourne. Most of the people in the suburb where I lived worked in either Nobels or Monsanto. In subsequent years Australia began to manufacture the Holden automobile, which, I am told by an acquaintance here who is into cars, can now be purchased in this country.

But there was also something else that struck me as odd, though it does not today have such force – the emotional attachment to England. Thus my landlady, who was a third-generation Australian, referred to her daughter's visit to England as 'going over home'.

Australia's history began at the beginning of the nineteenth century as a one-time penal colony when all of it was called New South Wales – now the name of only one of the states – to which felons were transported up until the 1860s and subject to the death penalty if they ever returned to England when freed. Only one unfortunate is known to have been hanged for doing so. Few of them would have wanted to, as most after freedom had far better lives in the colony.

Even though by the last years of transportation most arrivals were not convicts, the stigma persisted – until some years ago, when, for some reason, it became perversely fashionable to boast of convict forebears, to the extent that a teenage girl got into trouble for wanting to impress her schoolmates by altering the birth certificates of her predecessors to make them out as having been convicts! However, what even this schoolgirl would have wanted to remain forgotten is that it was not only male wrongdoers who were transported, but female, and that furthermore, most of the women had been prostitutes. That is not why they had been transported, since they had mostly been found guilty of thieving but, of course, being thieves, they had, almost certainly, also been prostitutes. Unlike the male convicts they did not have to serve two years before they were freed but got their freedom if they married before that.

There was such a shortage of women in early Australia that when a ship arrived transporting convict women a huge crowd of ex-convict men would greet it at the quayside, offering them marriage, shouting out how big their sheep farms were as if they were bidding at an auction. The good-looking women went first, of course, but even the plain ones had no trouble getting immediate husbands – and freedom. It is said that these ex-prostitutes went on to make excellent wives and mothers, a fact not liked by prudes and puritans such as a much later certain Australian senator renowned for his baleful influence in enforcing his own narrow-minded morals on laws and regulations. He was therefore understandably much put out when somebody researched his family tree and found that he was descended from a female convict who had almost certainly been a prostitute back home!

There might today be a further reason for not wishing to know too much about one's antecedents. This is connected with the huge influx of immigrants after the Second World War, in which Australia had had a bad scare. The Japanese had overrun New Guinea to the north of Australia, which consequently felt in danger of invasion. The fear was needless – the Japanese were already severely overstretched – but this was not known at the time and it induced a drive to increase the population after the war. The 'ten pound' immigration scheme in the British Isles on which I went to Australia was considered to be not bringing in enough people, so they turned to Europe. But the French do not emigrate at all, the Italians prefer the US, and so on. So Australia looked to the camps in which there were still millions of 'displaced' persons unable to return to their own countries for political reasons. Here the Australians were more able to pick and choose than with the British, for whom the age limit was fifty, whereas with them it was thirty-five and the medical was stricter. These Poles, Bulgarians, Yugoslavs and so on talked to each other in their common lingua franca – German. There were so many of them that, working among them, I picked up quite a bit of German, of which all I now remember are words like *der Australier* for 'Australian' and the phrase 'Ich bin ein Irischer Einwanderer' – I am an Irish immigrant (to let them know I wasn't English - i.e. not a whingeing Pom). But not all of them had been forced to work for the Germans, so it didn't do to enquire too closely what side they had on been on. I once, after returning to the UK, met a young Australian who refused to believe me when I told him that when I was in Melbourne the train announcements in Flinders Street station were repeated in German, because there were so many German-speaking displaced persons, or 'DPs' as they were disparagingly called. The more polite term was 'New Australians'. They were somewhat discriminated against. Adverts for rooms would say 'No New Australians'. Of course, today they will have been fully absorbed and will in turn be themselves discriminating against the latest wave of immigrants – from Hong Kong. This would have been impossible in my time there when there was an official 'whites only' immigration policy.

But the biggest change since I was there was brought about by Britain joining the European Economic Community. Up till then Australians were also British citizens. But British membership of the EEC meant that Australia, being outside it, was now a foreign country, and its citizens wishing to visit Britain were subject to all the rules which that entailed: passports, visas, work permits, length of stay, etc, and of course the same the other way. There was the case of a British doctor in an Australian hospital, served with a deportation order because he had forgotten to renew his work permit. He was doing such good work that there was an outcry, forcing the Australian government to rescind the order, but too late – he was already back in England and so disgusted he refused to return. People like my one-time third-generation Australian landlady who still referred to England as 'Home' must have turned in their graves.

Micks and Prods

I was once, briefly, a London member of the Communist Party. Well, I was young at the time and a girl I fancied was a member (and of course there had been that other time in Belfast when I had sung hymns at two Salvation Army services for the same reason). At one party branch meeting we were instructed to pass unanimously the resolution 'British rule should be withdrawn from Northern Ireland' presented by a member of the fraternal Irish Connolly Association. What about the million Northern Protestants who want to stay British? I asked. The Connolly man was taken aback, as indeed were the comrades, at so unexpected a question. After some angry exchanges with the Connolly man I walked out and never went back.

I learnt then the great difference between London Irish Nationalists and Scottish and Welsh Nationalists with whom I also came into contact. The Welsh and the Scots know they have to argue a case – not least to their own countrymen – and are therefore very practised at it. The Catholic Irish, however, believe that the case for a united Ireland is so manifestly obvious, so patently self-evident, that they are outraged at being asked to argue it, especially in left-wing circles. It was always the same. They never would discuss the Northern Protestants. No matter how I brought up the Protestants, they would only talk about the British ... the British ... the British. I was told that there weren't a million of them, that that was British propaganda, that if the British stopped brainwashing them they would go back to their Irish roots. I recall thinking I had at last convinced a nationalist that the million Northern Protestants were not a British problem but an *Irish* problem. But then he came out with what he believed to be the clincher trumping my argument. Of course they were a British problem, he claimed, since *the British had brought them there in the first place!*

Do Northern Protestants consider themselves Irish? Yes – even hardline Orangemen wear a shamrock on St Patrick's Day – but not *politically*. There was a time when they would not have made such a distinction. Anybody born on the island of Ireland was happy, indeed proud, to be Irish, whether Catholic or Protestant. Even the Anglo-Irish gentry with English public school accents had no more problem with being both Irish and British than the Welsh or the Scots. In the early 1900s the most famous Irishman in the world was the celebrated British playwright George Bernard Shaw, who was of an Irish Protestant family. But that changed with the 1916 Easter Uprising in the south and the creation of what is now called the Republic of Ireland in the south and British Northern Ireland with its million Protestants. The Catholic Nationalists succeeded in making *Irish* mean *Catholic* to the rest of the world. Every Northern Protestant who has emigrated will have experienced it being assumed that since he is Irish he must be Catholic. I recall a Labour Party man who, hearing my Belfast accent, assumed I would be pleased to be told that the British should get out of Northern Ireland. When I told him otherwise, he was annoyed. 'Oh, you're one of them,' he said. Yes, *them*, the million Protestants who complicate what Catholic Ireland believes to be the simple solution to the Irish problem: 'British Out'. I recall another Labour Party meeting where a London Irish member referred contemptuously to the Protestant Unionists with the words 'British Irish "ha ha"' as if that was such an absurd contradiction in terms as to be laughable. I said to the chairman, who was Welsh, 'Mr

Chairman, do you find it an absurd contradiction to be "British Welsh"? Lloyd George, the famous prime minister, obviously had no problem about being British even though his first language was Welsh. So why should I have a problem?' But while nobody tried to refute this I got no support either.

The Englishman Alistair Cooke, in his famous weekly broadcasts from America, related an anecdote about a prominent American senator of his acquaintance, proud of being well informed, who refused to believe that the majority of people in Northern Ireland were Protestants until Cooke proved it to him with an encyclopaedia reference book Cooke spotted on the well-informed senator's own bookshelf! Is it any wonder that the Northern Protestants every twelfth of July bang drums, march behind banners, light bonfires, to try to counter the belief held by the rest of the world that Irish means Catholic?

The sixteenth-century Plantation of Ulster, as it is called, was undoubtedly a cruel affair. Native Irish Catholics were brutally expelled from their lands to make way for Protestant Scottish and English settlers. But it is not reversible, any more than the cruel expulsion of north American Indians from the prairies or the aborigines from the sheep pastures of Australia. But deep down in the psyche of Catholic Ireland this has never been fully accepted. Thus, when I once argued with a London Irishman that a united Ireland would only be realised if enough of the million Northern Protestants could be persuaded not to vote to stay British, and he said that they had no right to be pro British, he really meant – deep down – that they had no right to be there at all.

Although there had been emigration to America from Ireland before the mid nineteenth century, Irish America - one of the most powerful forces in American politics - was mostly created by the Great Famine in Ireland in the 1840s. A million people starved to death and two million fled to America in its immediate aftermath, with continuing departures over many years. Ireland is probably the only country in the world whose population is less today at five million than it was in the eighteenth century when it was eight million.

The famine was caused by the potato crop being ruined by blight. The potato is the most nutritious vegetable in the world, so rich in vitamins that it can in itself provide a completely healthy diet - a not unmixed blessing. Many of the Irish ate nothing else and starved without it. It is a terrible stain on British history that the government in London did little to send relief. Oats (a staple food of the Northern Protestants) and wheat crops were unaffected and indeed had bumper crops: carts full of grain trundled past cabins in which families were dying of hunger. British government indifference constituted the most colossal callousness and was to cost it dear. The two million Irish who fled from the famine to America took with them a bitter anti-British hatred that lasts to this day among Irish Americans. The most hardline rebel in the 1916 rebellion was de Valéra with his Irish American connections. He fought a civil war against the peace treaty allowing the six counties to stay British and is said to have had a hand in the assassination of the republican leader Michael Collins for having negotiated it. He kept Eire neutral in the Second World War and sent condolences to the German embassy on the death of Hitler. In 1940, when Britain was fighting alone against Nazi Germany and in danger of invasion, the biggest demonstration New York has ever seen was of one hundred thousand Irish Americans proclaiming support for Germany, addressed by Hitler's ambassador. This of course died down when America entered the war but came back when the war was over. In the years of the Troubles, the IRA was largely funded from Irish America and when the violence was ended by the Good Friday Agreement, Gerry Adams and Martin McGuinness had to rush to America to sell it to the Irish Americans, which, it is reported, was harder than selling it to the IRA itself and not entirely successful. The continuing bomb outrages by the 'dissident IRA' or 'Real IRA' are almost certainly sponsored by Irish America. British government callousness in the Great Famine is still exacting its cost.

When my novel *The Last Romantic Out of Belfast* was brought out by a Belfast publisher, it was handled by a young woman editor. She was a lapsed Protestant whose partner was the Catholic poet Damian Gorman. They brought out a magazine called *Belfast Review* which published one of my short stories from an impending book collection. I later saw him on TV where he was filmed back-packing in Mexico. When he came to a village where there was a lively religious festival with effigies, fireworks and drinking, he told a Mexican in a bar 'I too come from a Catholic country'. In fact he comes from Northern Ireland, and at the time was living near Ballymena, the heartland of the Presbyterian Protestants, where he would have had people all around him with names like Cameron, MacDonald, Campbell... They could have quoted their bible at him, 'None so blind as they who do nor wish to see'.

This great blind spot of Catholic Ireland was illustrated by the Irish Senator who claimed that without British brainwashing the Northern Protestants would return to their Irish roots. I thought of my mother's side of the family who came from Ahoghill near Ballymena where I spent some of my school holidays and listened to the old people there who still spoke some broad Scots. To this day I can still understand quite a bit of Robbie Burns' poetry without a glossary.

Ca canny wi that. Be careful with that.
Dinna fash yersel mon. Don't upset yourself man.
A wheen o' wee yins. A lot of children.

Irish roots?

De Valera, Irish prime minister, was perhaps the prime example of this blind spot when he proclaimed it his ambition to make Ireland *the most Catholic country in the world.* If he had meant only his part of Ireland - Eire, now the Republic, it could be said that he realised it. Not only does the Irish Catholic Church dominate the education system and the health system but until recently imposed a censorship on books which banned James Joyce. But when de Valera spoke of Ireland he meant the whole island. How could he not, being such a hard line Republican? So how could he think that the whole island with its million Northern Protestants could be *the most Catholic country in the world*? Could he, or for that matter any Catholic Nationalist really believe what a Catholic Irish Londoner once told my (English) wife was the simple solution to the million Protestants: 'Ah sure we'd marry into them and get the children'.

The Irish Protestants are mostly represented in literature by southerners - from Dean Swift to Shaw. Northern Protestants have a poor showing, so that the very term 'Irish writer' is taken by the world to mean Catholic writer, as indeed it mostly does. One Northern Protestant to reach world status, the Belfast-born poet Louis MacNeice, is compromised by his English public-school education (he was the son of a bishop) and the fact that he subsequently lived all his life in England, so that his very Irishness – for ever paraded by him in his radio broadcasts in his English public-school accent – is questionable. There is no doubt that writers from the Protestant community come under great pressure, even though it is unspoken, to be sympathetic to nationalism. In meeting other Irish writers – even on just a social occasion – the other writers will be mostly Catholic whom the Protestant writers will not wish to offend.

Connor Cruise O'Brien, the well-known political commentator, has referred to this pressure. He aroused controversy by his claim that Northern Protestants will be accorded the status of 'honorary Catholic' if they renounce Britishness, however indirectly. Thus the Protestant poet, the late James Simmons, whose grandfather was Lord Mayor of Derry, wrote in a biographical piece about his childhood 'in the colony'. That word 'colony' would certainly have earned him 'honorary Catholic' status. A Protestant writer such as myself who prefers to be British is considered – even by other Protestant writers – to be outside the fellowship of the Irish writing community. In reviews I have been referred to as a Unionist writer even though Unionists are part of the British Conservative Party and I am moderately left wing, showing how the Catholic/ Protestant divide in Northern Ireland distorts what is no problem for the British Scots and the British Welsh.

The Orange Order gets a bad press, some of it deserved. Bowler-hatted bigots parading with flutes and drums and

King Billy banners to intimidate Catholic neighbourhoods and so on. Well, let me say something a bit more positive about them. My mother told me a story about her father, an Orange lodge master. Sometime in the 1920s the IRA shot and killed a high-ranking policeman as he was coming out of a church service in Lisburn Cathedral. Sectarian rioting broke out with Catholics being burned out of their houses. A Catholic woman and her children came to my grandmother's house and asked her to take them in, having been turned away from other Protestant houses. My grandmother said, 'No, you are not coming into our house, *we* are going into yours'. When the mob arrived at the woman's house my grandmother was standing in her doorway and beside her was my grandfather in his bowler hat, orange sash and white gloves, arms folded across his chest.

The neighbourhood I grew up in was mixed, with most Protestants on good terms with their Catholic neighbours, and I was brought up to respect Catholics' political beliefs. They have their big days and we have ours, I was taught. They would like a united Ireland but they know that, as long as we don't want it they can't have it, or at least, good Catholics do, those who, in the words often used, 'were not bitter like the Falls Road'.

It was only when I emigrated to Australia on the 'ten pounds scheme' that I discovered that things were not like that at all. I was living in Melbourne for about a year when my mother wrote to me that one of our Catholic neighbours was going to Melbourne. Widower Harry was very well liked by even the most true-blue Loyalist of his neighbours, he was so helpful and obliging. He was, as they say, very good with his hands, unlike some men, who, their wives said scathingly, couldn't change a light bulb. Harry could change a washer on a dripping tap, ease a sticking door, clear a blocked drain. He had come to my mother's rescue when my father made a mess of trying to fix a loose window frame. He seemed a perfect example of a 'not bitter like the Falls Road' Catholic.

He was living with his son in Melbourne, who had married an Australian, and at first my visit to him went well. I cannot remember why there was quite a crowd at his son's place. It had a big garden and I was for some reason indoors at an open window, from which I overheard Harry outside talking to a group of Australians about Northern Ireland. I still remember his words as he told them, 'The British occupation of North Ireland is no different to the German occupation of France in the war'. I was so shocked I moved away, not wanting to hear any more.

Was this the same 'not-bitter-like-the-Falls Road' Harry so much liked by his Protestant neighbours? The same Harry who was on the friendliest terms with the most true-blue Loyalist family in the neighbourhood, whose menfolk were not only all Orangemen who 'walked on the twelfth' but who flew the Union Jack on every official occasion, in whose house Harry would often be laughing and joking over a cup of tea, facing a wall with a big picture of royalty on it, flanked by another of King Billy crossing the Boyne on his white horse?

'... no different to the German occupation of France in the war...' Harry had described his homeland – and mine. I still remember that day in Australia when I learnt that the Catholic/Protestant divide in the society I grew up in was far greater than I had been led to believe.

The Great 'What If?'

There are some events that are so important that it is impossible to imagine what subsequent history would have been like if they had not happened, and so they seem as though bound to have happened, as if inevitable, like evolution itself.

Take the event drummed into every schoolboy: the Battle of Hastings, or '1066 and all that'. The 'All That' included the emergence of the English language, not just of vital importance for Britain but for the whole world in its history and its literature. Not just Britain but America without the English language is impossible to imagine.

But was the outcome of the Battle of Hastings inevitable? Far from it. Indeed, it was, to borrow the words of the Duke of Wellington about another important battle, Waterloo, 'a damned close-run thing'. How do we know? Because we have the word for that from no less than the winner – William the Conqueror himself.

Before we look at the battle itself let us look at its precursors. William was what in Ireland would be called a 'chancer'. His invasion of the south coast of England took advantage of Harold having to deal with an invasion in the north of England by the army of Harold Hadrada, the King of Norway, whom he easily defeated but had to immediately hurry south in forced marches to face the Normans. Even so, he got there fast enough to occupy the best position at the top of the hill, from which the formidable Saxon infantry were able to beat back the Norman cavalry over the course of nearly a whole day.

You can visit the village of Battle in Sussex where the substantial ruin of an abbey which William built is still there with the altar to mark the spot where the battle turned and gave William his, as he put it, 'great deliverance' – the spot where the Anglo-Saxon King Harold was killed by an arrow from a volley of arrows shot into the sky by the Normans to fall down upon the Saxons, one piercing Harold's eye. But that could have happened only because Harold, for some reason, was looking upwards. Even then, for it to hit him exactly in his eye was an unlikely coincidence, rather than striking bone, which, while it would have wounded him, would not have caused his instant death, which was what so threw the Saxon army into panic and confusion. No wonder William built an abbey to give thanks for his great deliverance. He of all people would have been the first to agree that the Battle of Hastings was a 'damned close-run thing'.

In July 1944 a bomb went off at a conference between Hitler and his generals. The bomb was placed behind what the plotters had every reason to believe was simply the middle leg of the five legs on each side of the conference table. But there was in fact a thick panel behind that leg which ran across the table. While those on the bomb side of the panel were killed, those on the other side of the panel, including Hitler, were only wounded.

Why the table had been made with that panel is not known; the stout legs were perfectly adequate to support it. There was no reason why the plotters should have had that table looked at underneath to check for anything that would hinder the effect of their bomb. It need not have mattered on which side of the table leg the bomb was placed. Hitler's life was saved by an unforeseeable quirk of carpentry.

So what if Hitler *had* been killed, as he almost certainly should have been?

It has been speculated that the conspirators, who included some of Hitler's top generals, would have ended the war earlier. If so, then some of the bloodiest fighting and heaviest casualties, especially on the eastern front, would have been avoided. In July 1944 German morale, both military and civilian, was still high, despite the air raids on cities. Germans told each other confidently that Hitler would launch a deadly secret weapon that would defeat the enemy, and indeed the rocket attacks on London in 1944 and 1945, which took everybody by surprise, affected the spirit of Londoners far more than the previous Blitz. The earlier end of the European conflict would have meant the earlier transfer of forces to the Pacific and the earlier defeat of Japan. And, perhaps, more than anything else, at least a million Jews – some say far more – would have survived the Holocaust.

So much would have been different if a table had been supported only by its legs in the normal way:

For want of a nail a shoe was lost.
For want of a shoe a horse was lost.
For want of a horse a battle was lost.
For want of a battle a kingdom was lost.

So many great events in history have depended on chance trivialities as if on the tossing of a coin.

Feet of Clay

Sir Isaac Newton

The poet Alexander Pope wrote a famous couplet about Newton: 'Nature and nature's laws were cloaked in night, And then came Newton and all was light.' This man of the seventeenth century was one of the greatest figures there has ever been in science and mathematics. When the rocket engineers calculate the paths and orbits of satellites they are using Newton's equations governing gravity. Children are still delighted to be told the (probably mythical) story of him seeing the apple falling from the tree and deciding to explore why it fell and the rules of its falling. When Einstein found that some of his equations about relativity did not quite agree with Newton's equations, he altered them to make them agree. He later found that he need not have (gravity behaves slightly differently the further out we go in the universe), but it shows the awe in which he is held even by people like Einstein.

So what kind of man was this scientific giant whose shadow still falls over us?

He was foul-tempered and quarrelsome, superstitious, believed in alchemy, was deeply religious and wrote treatises on the prophesies of Daniel in the Bible and on the Book of Revelation. He was made Master of the Mint as a sinecure to give him a living but insisted on exercising the power it gave him regarding forgery which carried the death penalty. When people appealed to him to spare the life of a young forger about whose offence there were extenuating circumstances, he refused and when the public hanging was carried out he cackled with glee. Everybody is agreed that Newton the man was a thoroughly nasty specimen.

Richard Wagner

Wagner occupies a place in the pantheon of composers that is different to that of the others. Many of them had their quirks of personality, of course. Handel liked his beer. Mozart rowed with his wife and was reckless with money. Beethoven was rowdy, untidy, arrogant and badly dressed.

But these are failings that we can all sympathise with, indeed which many of us share. Not so with Wagner's anti-semitism, however much music lovers try to play it down by equating it with the casual anti-semitism we hear even the nicest people come out with. (Thus I remember friends of ours telling us a story about hearing a couple in a restaurant query something in their bill; 'They looked Jewish,' our progressive, slightly left-wing friends explained, and were annoyed when I asked them why they thought only Jews would challenge a bill.) But Wagner's anti-Semitism was of a different order. He was Hitler's favourite composer and it was not only his music that Hitler admired. Unfortunately for Wagner's apologists he was also a prolific correspondent and many of his letters have survived. Some of them contain the most gross and virulent anti-Semitism. In one of them he asks: 'How could a *Jew* be a great composer?' Had he been around during the Nazi era it is more than probable that he would not only have returned Hitler's admiration but would have approved of the Holocaust.

Leo Tolstoy

It is something of a mystery why we know so little about Shakespeare the man, when, for example, so much more is known about not only his contemparaties, like Inigo Jones or Christopher Marlowe, but about Geoffrey Chaucer, who lived two hundred years earlier. But perhaps disappointment at this should be tempered with the thought that it is maybe just as well. Tolstoy is considered such a giant in world literature that his readers do not like to be told about his darker side, such as his having been a youth who regularly raped the serf girls on his parents' great estate, as referred to in my essay titled *Rape*. They may also not like to be reminded about some of his other little foibles.

He attacked religion, Shakespeare, inherited wealth. He claimed to be penniless, making over his estate to his wife – whom, of course, he dominated – and 'living the life of a peasant under her roof'. This poor peasant life meant him coming in from the fields stinking of manure as he sat down to eat from silver plates, attended by a liveried footman in a powdered wig.

When he left his long-suffering wife to meditate in a humble dwelling his simple needs included being attended by his personal physician.

Maxim Gorky, another famous though much younger Russian writer, was also a great admirer of Tolstoy. He eagerly took up the opportunity to meet Tolstoy in his old age, while holidaying at a Black Sea resort. He wished he had not. Whereas Gorky wanted to talk about Tolstoy's books and Russian literature, all Tolstoy wanted to talk about was men's sexual urges, and in the grossest way. How often did Gorky have a woman? He cocked his arm up from his elbow to symbolise the male erection and wanted to know when Gorky last had his cock up a nice fanny. Gorky was appalled. Could this be the great author of *Anna Karenina* and *War and Peace*, this foul-mouthed old lecher? Surely nature had played a trick on us?

Gorky might have asked the same question about Newton and Wagner. But Gorky was wrong. Nature does not play tricks. Nature is blind. When nature showers her gifts and talents, in science, music, literature, upon humanity, she does so blindly indifferent as to the kind of individuals on whom they accidentally fall.

The Rising Standards of the Poor

Food. Clothing. Shelter. The three basic human needs by which standards of living have been measured since before the Stone Age. Yet even in comparatively recent times their order of priority has changed. I was a child in the 1930s. I was born into the upper working class, a term no longer used, but which was perfectly meaningful then. My father was a bespoke shoemaker, I had one uncle, a tailor, another a railway engine driver, and another in charge of a railway signal box, i.e. all of them skilled artisans who, even during the terrible depression of the 1930s, did not suffer anything like what the unskilled went through: the dole, and, worst of all, the humiliating means tests in which officials would search people's houses and demand to know how a wife or daughter could afford such nice underwear.

Indeed, my father and two of my uncles were, even during the worst depression the world has ever known, buying their houses on mortgages. But part of that was because houses then were very much cheaper, costing only about four hundred pounds, which even after adjusting into today's money would be a fraction of what those houses would cost now. But food and clothes were much dearer. Poverty in those days meant ragged clothes and ill nourishment, and for children, bare feet in summer. Even luckier children like me had to wear our older brothers' out-grown clothes and when we came home from school we had to change into old clothes before going out to play. Our fathers had 'Sunday best' clothes that they did not wear every day, a term that no longer has any meaning.

Back street children I went to school with seemed to live on bread and margarine, with fish and chips a greatly esteemed luxury. On the other hand the back street slum houses they lived in were let at dirt-cheap rents.

Since then there has been a huge rise in what, for want of a better term, is the standard of living of poverty. A recent TV programme was about the hardships of families living on benefits. What struck me, and, I would have thought, many ex-working-class people of my generation, was how neatly dressed and well-nourished the children looked, compared to how they would have looked when I was a child. I hasten to add that that is a very good thing and a welcome sign of an improved society. Yet it is difficult to sympathise with, for instance, the single mother who was being advised how to make her money go further, and was outraged at the idea of using charity shops in which very good quality – indeed sometimes new – unwanted children's clothes are sold very cheaply. In fact, charity shop staff themselves say that their customers are mostly middle class.

But it is not only in what are called advanced countries, such as ours, that this huge improvement in the standard of living of the poor has taken place. Haiti is one of the poorest countries in the world and featured in the news recently when it was struck by an earthquake and aid had to be rushed to it. I was struck by the appearance of the people in the long queues for the food handouts. No ragged or patched clothes to be seen. It was the same story in another TV item about Mumbai in India. The slums looked dreadful yet the swarms of children seemed well-nourished and were all neatly dressed in jeans and T-shirts. The same was true in the shanty towns of Rio de Janeiro or even, in the worst case, in China, where an open sewer ran down a street of corrugated tin shacks in a village, yet the children seemed well-nourished, wearing neat jeans, trainers and T-shirts.

Of course there is always a down side to even the best of things. When poverty in the working class meant ragged clothes and ill-nourishment, this did not in itself cause any shame or social stigma. Those ragged back street children I went to the elementary school with were not looked down on by us better-dressed and better-fed ones. Because we were all working class. It is different today, and not only here. A recent survey in America showed how most people now regard themselves as middle class, and have consequently taken middle class attitudes on board, which includes regarding having money difficulties as something shameful to be hidden behind the lace curtains. It would be the same here. On a recent TV documentary, working-class parents affected by unemployment told of how their child would be made to feel embarrassed if their parents could not afford to send them on a two day school trip to France. Oh, the shame of it! In my day we were lucky to get a Sunday school excursion to the nearest seaside with tea and buns in a church hall.

We have certainly come a long way since I went to junior school. I recall our teacher asking those of us in the class to put our hands up if we could get the money for our new reader so she could know how many would need to get the old used ones for free.

I was a scholarship boy. But the grammar school I went to has left little lasting impression on me. When I think of my schooldays it is that rough, tough working-class junior school that I remember with affection and gratitude.